D0142615

THE
DECLINE OF
THRIFT
IN AMERICA

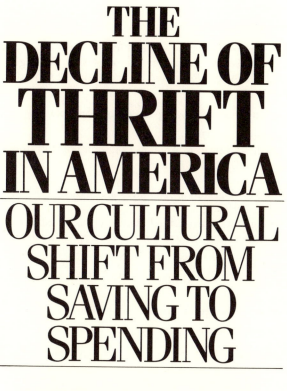

THE DECLINE OF THRIFT IN AMERICA

OUR CULTURAL SHIFT FROM SAVING TO SPENDING

DAVID M. TUCKER

New York
Westport, Connecticut
London

339.43
T89d

Copyright Acknowledgment

The author and publisher are grateful for permission to reprint from
Collected Poems, Second Edition by Conrad Aiken. Copyright © 1953,
1970 by Conrad Aiken. Reprinted by permission of Oxford University
Press, Inc.

Library of Congress Cataloging-in-Publication Data

Tucker, David M., 1937–
    The decline of thrift in America : our cultural shift from saving
to spending / David M. Tucker.
        p.   cm.
    Includes bibliographical references and index.
    ISBN 0-275-93685-6
    1. Saving and thrift—United States—History—20th century.
    2. Consumer credit—United States—History—20th century.
    I. Title.
    HG7920.T83   1991
    339.4'3—dc20   90-7421

British Library Cataloguing-in-Publication Data is available.

Library of Congress Catalog Card Number: 90–7421
ISBN: 0–275–93685–6

First published in 1991

Praeger Publishers, One Madison Avenue, New York, NY 10010
An imprint of Greenwood Publishing Group, Inc.

Printed in the United States of America

∞
The paper used in this book complies with the
Permanent Paper Standard issued by the National
Information Standards Organization (Z39.48–1984).

10 9 8 7 6 5 4 3 2 1

Contents

Preface

Americans' long-running affair with the virtue of thrift apparently ended in the affluent 1950s, when we killed the concept and removed the term, if not from dictionaries, at least from current language, textbooks, and reference books. By then, the theory and practice of thrift had been in decay for at least a generation. Advertising, consumer credit, and a self-indulgent psychology had been eroding the practice since the 1920s, and the Great Depression of the 1930s had provided economists with a reasonable justification for relabeling thrift as the contemptible vice which threw sand in the gears of our consumer economy. By the 1960s, even the public schools had dropped the teaching of frugality and thrift.

In the generation since declaring thrift obsolescent, Americans have shown little remorse. And yet the energy crisis of the 1970s and the decline of industrial productivity that has demoted Americans from first to no better than a slipping sixth place in per capita income has led a few opinion makers to talk of a "Toyota shock" turning attention to Japanese industrial productivity, education, and occasionally even to their rates of national saving. In the 1970s, the Japanese saved some 20 percent of their income while we banked about 6 percent. In the 1980s, our rate fell to below 4 percent. Thrift is no obsolescent virtue if the nation is concerned with preserving a standard of living.

Prodigality seems an inevitable product of prosperity. Once economic superiority is achieved, the virtues of production give way to the ethic of consumption. America is following the classic rise and decline of Britain. Our thriftlessness is an American strain of the disease that destroyed the economic leadership of the United Kingdom, decaying its industries and diminishing its standard of living. When Britain's bourgeois spirit of thrift, industry, efficiency, and concern for technology and productivity succumbed to antibourgeois culture, its decline was inevitable. Americans today are far along the antibourgeois pathology that Britain suffered. We are at the very bottom of national savings and investment charts for the industrial world.

The Decline of Thrift in America is a study of these long-neglected American values of frugality and thrift. It is a story told by a historian who believes the study of culture offers much insight and wisdom. Values have been more than private choices; American culture has sought uniformity, insisting that all believe and practice the right, the good, the desirable behavior. The United States was born in a thrift culture which continued its dominance for more than a century, a culture insisting on frugality as the best means for promoting the general welfare. Americans responded to the general culture by saving about 15 percent of their income. In the twentieth century, after consumption gained control of the culture and promoted spending as best for the common good, the personal savings rate dropped by half. In the 1980s, fewer than half of American families were saving money.

How individuals handle dollars has always been subject to community pressure, a reality often ignored by economists even though they have no persuasive explanation for the collapse of saving in America. Cultural historians easily explain that individual spending, as well as government policy, reflects the dominant culture. But economists have little patience with a cultural explanation because it places levers of control outside the easy reach of policy makers. Unlike the money supply or interest rate—which are easily altered by the Federal Reserve Board—culture has no gear for a quick shift into reverse. No lever can change the values of a nation in a year or even a decade. Yet, cultural attitudes are more decisive determinants of savings rates and standards of living than any policy tool of government. Understanding the attitudes of a people can be more enlightening than charting levels of employment or percentages of growth in a money supply.

The story of frugality and thrift opens a large window on the American past, revealing our national character as tradition, religion, education, and capitalism promoted a virtue which asked us to restrain ourselves and trade real pleasures of the moment for the possibility of better experiences in the future. Private virtues and habits are, to be sure, difficult for outsiders to observe directly. But the handling of money has been a major cultural concern, and public records provide ample evidence from which to create a picture—with colorful detail of ethnicity, religion, and individual personality—illustrating the diversity of the culture of thrift. The decline of that culture began in the late nineteenth century with an angry American protest against thrifty Chinese immigrants. This led to a great cultural reversal, undercutting the old virtue and promoting the new ideal of a higher standard of living supported by spending, consumption, and debt.

A renewed appreciation of the national value of thrift is essential for the future well-being of our economy. But even if we are unable to restore the old positive definition of frugality, at least the history of thrifty ancestors can be a precious memory to treasure as we struggle to survive with a sharply reduced standard of living.

1

Traditional Thrift

The moral history of frugality and thrift extends back no more than ten thousand years. In its first two million years, humanity may have been less thrifty than the squirrels and chipmunks, the ants and bees, in hoarding away surplus food for cold and barren seasons. Hunting-gathering tribes who migrated in pursuit of food could not become accumulators. They feasted when the earth was bountiful and suffered famine when the land turned hostile. Only after humans invented agriculture did they settle down in villages and accumulate a surplus. Farmers learned to gather and store surplus food and to save part for seed. Frugality and thrift—saving seeds for spring planting— were essential for survival in hostile climates with alternating seasons.

In a world of scarcity, tribal survival required inculcation of the habits of thrift and industry. Those who neither worked nor saved contributed nothing to the community food supply: improvident individuals weakened the community. The advocacy of tribal survival virtues is preserved in the wisdom literatures of folk maxims: "Take a lesson from the ants, you lazy fellow. Learn from their ways and be wise! For though they have no king to make them work, yet they labor hard all summer, gathering food for the winter" (Proverbs 6:6–9). And: "The wise man saves for the future, but the foolish man spends whatever he gets" (Proverbs 21:20). The persistence of tribal wisdom among agricultural peasants is also found in other literatures. Consider the advice of the Greek poet Hesiod: "Do not put your work off til tomorrow and the day after; for a sluggish worker does not fill his barn, nor one who puts off his work."[1] Exhortations to work and store away a surplus are common to all ancient literatures.

The tribal concepts of work and thrift required only that a living sufficiency, not an excess, be acquired. Excess provisions would only spoil where no market existed. Once sufficient food for survival was obtained, further effort seemed pointless. Contentment with the minimum, rather than acquisitiveness, dominated tribal thinking. Village workers would not compete for prestige with material symbols—dress, housing, or food—lest they arouse envy, jealousy, and anger. Rather, primitives looked and acted alike, and their work habits would be characterized as "lazy" by people in developed civilizations. The customs of ancient humans did not include the practice of working for gain.[2]

Tribal communities must have practiced work habits similar to those of Chinese peasants observed by anthropologists in the 1940s. For these Chinese peasants, incentive ended once a subsistence was secured; farmers might then cease their labors and relax. Peasants sought no material riches, but labored only to meet their culture's low standard of consumption. As children, they learned the wisdom of simple living and the evil of extravagance. The child who expressed preferences or demands in food or clothes was scorned and beaten. To refuse food offered by elders brought swift punishment.[3] Peasant subsistence economies surely taught contentment and thrift. Neither consumption nor acquisition was considered prestigious in peasant economies.

Ceremonial occasions were the only exceptions to the peasant rule of frugality. Lavish feasts were required rituals for funerals and marriages, and perhaps the earliest saving of money was in preparation for these special celebrations. When money first entered the barter economy three thousand years ago, people must have seen the advantage of hoarding coins rather than perishable goods for future ceremonies. Certainly Chinese peasants hoarded their extra coins for these special times when the surplus could be spent in ritual extravagance. But lavish spending in celebration never spilled over into daily life in these economies of scarcity; the survival ethic of thrift controlled all but the special days.[4]

The rise of urban communities separated peoples from their traditional country ethics. Once Mediterranean peoples created urban civilizations, peasant frugality was eroded by a new consumption ethic. When abundance offered the choice, pleasure proved preferable to pain and self-restraint. After military conquests brought luxury, waste, and extravagance to Rome, a country-born fundamentalist, Cato, sought the office of censor in 184 B.C. A Roman military leader and senator, Cato championed the traditional virtues of frugality and restraint against luxury and extravagance. "No one recommended squeezing a penny more fervently than that self-appointed preacher of the old virtues . . . the elder Cato," asserts historian M. I. Finley. To restrain consumer extravagance, Cato taxed ornaments, women's clothing, and expensive vehicles at ten times their worth. Seeking to uphold old virtues of industry and frugality, he censored those who neglected their vineyards and wrote *De Agricultura* advising against wasted labor, time, or equipment. To make money from an estate, Cato insisted, an owner must be "a seller rather than a buyer."[5] Cato's peasant passion for frugality and self-sufficiency represented the traditional Roman mores which deteriorated in the urban empire.

Urban philosophers in ancient Greece and Rome omitted frugality from their system of ethics. Their four cardinal virtues— prudence, temperance, courage, and justice—did not specifically include frugality. Prudence might seem to suggest frugality and thrift, but the Latin word *prudens* actually meant exercising foresight, an awareness of the consequences of one's actions—and did not specifically include any economic consideration. Had classical ethics chosen to emphasize frugality, the virtue chosen would have been *parsimonia*, which specifically includes thrift, frugality, economy, and savings. The ancient urban philosophers could never endorse the frugality of Cato the censor. The nearest Aristotle and Plato came to endorsing savings was with the virtue of temperance, which included frugality as one of its meanings but really stressed the moral habit of avoiding extremes. Moderate prodigality would have been as reasonable to Aristotle as moderate thrift.

When Christianity converted the ancient world, urban values were demoted because they seemed evidence of the arrogant pride of pagans who believed their own reason might lead to good behavior. Christian ethics were based not on self-reliant human reason but on submission to the teachings of Jesus. Christians replaced the urban emphasis on classical virtues with a list of seven deadly vices—pride, envy, anger, unchastity, avarice, gluttony, dejection, weariness, and vainglory—sins against which each individual must struggle.[6]

Christianity taught a subsistence mentality much like that of the peasants. Acquiring wealth, accumulating more than what was necessary for bare subsistence, was severely condemned as an economic form of pride. The approved purpose of work was not capital accumulation but subsistence, avoidance of idleness, and financial support of the Church. From the ancient through the medieval world, Christianity condemned all hope of worldly progress, all credit, and especially all loans charging interest. Money lending fell to the Jews, who were regarded as "necessary and useful" but "hateful."[7]

Roman Jews demonstrated a commercial mentality quite different from their otherworldy Christian counterparts. Driven out of agriculture in the eighth century by the Moslems, Jews became an urban people who survived in the Islamic and Christian worlds by their handicrafts, peddling, commerce, and high finance. They moved beyond the traditional peasant understanding of thrift—accumulating a subsistence—to a capitalist ambition of saving money to purchase of an ever larger store of market goods and to lend out at interest. By the twelfth century, granting loans at interest of 33 percent or more had become the main occupation for Jews in Western Europe. Envy of Jewish wealth provoked Christians to anti-Semitic massacres and expulsions, but European kingdoms usually invited the expelled Jews to return because trade languished when Hebrews were banned.[8]

The Church fought a great battle against wealth—prohibiting

interest, exaltating poverty, advocating the just price and the fair wage, and upgrading the human vice of avarice to the very worst of the seven deadly sins. Avarice came to be depicted as a disgusting, small, crouching figure with money bags and a counting table. But the Church lost its battle: Christian lenders evaded the usury proscription by creating fictional sales and invented figures. The thirteenth-century scholastics finally accepted defeat by the urban market economy and opened a loophole—interest might be charged if the lender were running a risk or failing to gain. With reluctance, Roman Catholicism accepted the emerging capitalism of Renaissance Italy.[9]

Thirteenth-century Florence represented a new capitalist spirit of wealth accumulation. Leon Battista Alberti (1404–1471) stated "With money, one can have a town house or a villa, and all the trades and craftsmen will toil like servants for the man who has money. He who has none goes without everything, and money is required for every purpose." Teaching accumulation of wealth, Alberti instructed his Florentine children to "always remember, my sons, that your expenditure should never exceed your income." Surplus money saved in Florence could be invested for further gains. "If you have money," Paolo Certaldo said, "do not wait, do not keep it lying idle at home, for it is better to work in vain than to be idle for nothing, because even if you gain no profit by working, at least you do not lose the habit of doing business."[10] Striving for gain and considering time as money were part of the new Renaissance Florentine mentality.

The economic revolution in the great commercial centers displaced medieval religiosity with a new intellectual and literary perspective—labeled humanism—which refused to rank poverty above wealth. This secular perspective with its admiration of human achievement discredited the traditional Christian eulogy of the virtuous pauper. Advocates of the dignity of man—of the individual's capacity for personal improvement—naturally praised success, considered the accumulation of wealth a virtue, and demoted poverty to a vice. The poor were now stereotyped as disgraceful, able-bodied beggars who ought to be forced to work. Alberti declared that, "even the gods do not love the poor" and insisted that "it is better to die than to live in poverty." Living in destitution had become shameful for Renaissance man, who would strip even the mendicant friars of their dignity and force them to labor for their bread.[11] Humanists emancipated from Christian tradition found mendicant friars less admirable than capitalists.

The spirit of capitalism and the traditional habit of peasant thrift were antagonistic forces. Consider the example of Martin Luther, the German-born peasant who launched the conservative Reformation against the Roman Catholic Church's drift in economics and theology away from primitive Christianity. Luther hated affluence, luxury, and laxity in the church of Rome. He opposed not only papal indulgences, but also usury and the spirit of capitalism. He condemned high finance and commerce, declaring that "it would be a far more godly thing to increase agriculture and decrease commerce." His peasant interpretation of the Seventh Commandment—"Thou shalt not steal"—went far beyond theft and prohibited "greed, usury, overcharging, counterfeit goods, short measure," and perhaps even profitable commerce. Luther specifically urged men not to "run after gold."[12]

Luther was no model of thrift himself. His profligate giving would have impoverished the family but for his frugal wife Catherine who saved all she could hide from her husband. Yet he preached frugality to others. He advocated abolishing Church festivals and feasts because they encouraged the vices of "drinking, gambling, loafing, and all manner of sin. . . . " Luther complained that, as a result of saints' days, the typical German "neglect[ed] his work and spen[t] more money than he would otherwise." Eating and drinking were the special vices of Germans, he said, and this "waste of money" should stop. Luther spoke the language of his peasant-miner father when he applauded work and thrift as the exaltation of God. "As the bird is born to fly," he quoted Scripture, "so man is born to work" (Job 5:7). By advocating work and thrift, Luther unwittingly contributed to the commercial revolution he deplored.

The capitalist mentality Luther opposed had spread north from Italian cities and created one of the greatest economic shifts in history. The Italian cities had colonized northern Europe during the Middle Ages, bringing education and urbanization to the northern markets. Then the lower competitive costs—wages, transportation, and unbeatable industry—of the North made cities on the Atlantic the centers of world commerce. The economic shift came from material rather than spiritual causes. Consider the case of England, which rose to economic dominance in the North not because of its Protestant conversion, but probably because of its island location and the fact that its people had lived longer within the commercial market. Landless peasantry had already disappeared. Since the thirteenth century, the English had lived not in a traditional society of fixed status and place, but in a market economy. English peasants may have lived in mud huts in villages such as Wigston and practiced thrifty, self-sufficient farming, but they sold their small agricultural surplus at the Leicester market and used the money to buy necessities—salt and iron—or saved it to acquire more land. Over the centuries, a minority of acquisitive peasants gained distinctive wealth in this thrift economy. Where land sold freely, agricultural workers were free to move, and the individual might be independent of the group. English children left home as teenagers, moved to town or hired out as farm servants, and looked forward to saving enough to have farms of their own by age thirty. English individualism predates English Protestantism.[13]

In Old English, the word *thrift* signified a thriving condition or a means to prosperity. Linked with the word *husbandry* (much like the Greek *oeconomy*), thrift meant efficient household management. "Thrift and good husbandry" were commonly linked, as were "thriftiness and good housewifery." Good husbandry books included Thomas Tusser's thrift wisdom: "Son, think not thy money . . . to burn, but keep it for profit, to serve thine own turn. A fool and his money be soon at debate, which after, with sorrow, repents him too late." Thomas Tusser's *Five Hundred Points of Good Husbandry* (1557) recommends "The Ladder to Thrift":

> To take thy calling thankfully,
> and shun the path to beggary.
> To grudge in youth no drudgery,
> to come by knowledge perfectly,
> to count no travell slavery,
> that brings in penny saverly.

8

> To follow profit, earnestly,
> but meddle not with pilfery.[14]

Seventeenth-century England had grown so capitalist and commercial that poverty had become an embarrassment, bringing with it melancholy, ridicule, scorn, and friendlessness. Henry Peacham complained in *The Worth of a Peny or a Caution to keep Money* (1664) that poverty had lost its former association with piety. "*My son better it is to dy* than to be poor: for now Money is the world's god," he wrote. Money gave beauty, power, status, and honor. "Money's a Queen, that doath bestow Beauty and Birth, to High and Low." Without money, a sick man discovered that "the Doctor is not at leisure to visit you, yea hardly your neighbors, and familiar friends; but unto monied and rich men they fly as Bees to the willow palms. . . ." To prevent the misery of want, Peacham believed that, after religion, "thrift is the first thing we should teach our children." He recommended simplicity of dress, entertainment, and diet. "The truth is," he wrote, "that those men live the longest and are commonly in perfect health, who content themselves with the least and simplest meat, which not only saves the purse, but preserves the body. . . ." In addition to urging frugality, Peacham stressed industry as a means of avoiding poverty. "The times in no age," he wrote, "were so hard as to deny industry and ingenuity a livelyhood; the Soldier may live by the exercise of his sword as the scholler by the exercise of his pen. . . ."[15]

Among the London merchants of the 1620s (labeled mercantilists), concern for national wealth justified attacks on tobacco and alcohol consumption and fashions of dress. London merchant Thomas Mun criticized these wastes of the national treasure, writing that "the general leprosie of our Piping, Potting, Feasting, Fashions, and mis-spending of our time in Idleness and Pleasure . . . hath made us effeminate in our bodies, weak in our knowledge, poor in our Treasure, declined in our Valour, unfortunate in our Enterprises, and contumned by our Enemies."[16] The English should be as frugal as the Dutch, Mun argued, and then England would be a wealthy and powerful nation.

Frugality and thrift were promoted as national traits by seventeenth-century mercantilists. Modern political economy really began with the nationalistic assumption that the wealth of a nation depended on the frugality and industry of its citizens. Concern for national wealth led Mun to attack individual prodigality, the opposite of thrift. Prodigality was blamed for growing poverty in England. According to George Mackenzie's *The Moral History of Frugality* (1691), "If Frugality prevailed, it would open the Store-Houses of Charity, the Poor would be Fed, [and] the sick would be taken care of." Luxury and avarice consumed too much of the people's wealth, leaving too little for charity. According to Mackenzie, the English should return to their ancient frugality, to the time when they, like the Jews, were a frugal, industrious people who ate simple food. They should remember the New Testament instructions against luxury and avarice. Mackenzie accused Englishmen of growing less charitable as their imagined necessities increased.[17]

The world's best-known thrift essay came out of the eighteenth-century British Empire. While on a boat to England in 1757, the American colonist Benjamin Franklin penned his sixteen-page pamphlet, *The Way to Wealth*, which, with its pithy homilies—"God helps them that help themselves," and "Early to bed, and early to rise, makes a man healthy, wealthy, and wise"—recommended industry, frugality, and thrift.

If you would be wealthy . . . think of Saving as well as of Getting: The Indies have not made Spain rich, because her Outgoes are greater than her Incomes. . . . What maintains one Vice, would bring up two Children. You may think perhaps, That a little Tea, or a little Punch now and then, Diet a little more costly, Clothes a little finer, and a little Entertainment now and then, can be no great Matter; but remember what Poor Richards says. . . . Beware of little Expenses; a small Leak will sink a great Ship. . . . Buy what thou hast no Need of, and ere long thou shalt sell thy Necessaries.

Franklin also abhorred debt:

Think what you do when you run in Debt; *You give to another Power over your Liberty.* If you cannot pay at the Time, you will be ashamed to see your Creditor; you will be in Fear when you speak to him; you will make poor pitiful sneaking Excuses, and by Degrees come to lose your Veracity, and sink into base downright lying; for, as Poor Richard says, *The second Vice is Lying, the first is running in Debt....* Whereas a freeborn Englishman ought not to be ashamed or afraid to see or speak to any Man living. But Poverty often deprives a Man of all Spirit and Virtue: *'Tis hard for an empty Bag to stand upright.... The Borrower is a Slave to the Lender, and the Debtor to the Creditor,* disdain the Chain, preserve your Freedom; and maintain your independency: Be *industrious* and *free*; be *frugal* and *free*.[18]

The Way to Wealth repackaged traditional peasant thrift advice for the capitalist world. The phrasing is proverbial and folksy, but the message is no longer the old survival necessity which prevents the misery of want. Thrift had become the means of growing rich. "If you would be wealthy," Franklin wrote, "think of Saving as well as Getting...." The peasant world offered only limited possibilities, but Franklin's ever-expanding Atlantic economy offered constant getting. To exploit modern markets, the traditional ethic of limited work and frugality—moral habits practiced in backward Spain and Ireland—had to be replaced by constant industry, efficient use of time, and savings. Saving money was transformed by Franklin from a peasant trait into part of the middle-class ethic—industry, frugality, and thrift—which economic individualism prescribed as the means to fulfill the hopes of individuals and their nations.

Franklin's thrift advice emancipated savings from religious restraint. His *Way to Wealth* was a morally neutral handbook of economic life. If one desired wealth, these were the steps to success, but Franklin offered no moral judgement on the wisdom of pursuing riches. In his own life, Franklin never actually endorsed greed even though as a young man he abandoned organized religion for what could almost pass for the Protestant ethic. He compiled his own list of thirteen virtues and cultivated one each week, seeking by resolve and steady practice to turn the virtues into regular habits. The list he sought to live by included temperance, frugality, and industry—but not charity.[19]

In his life, as in his list of virtues, Franklin never made wealth the only pursuit. He seems to have believed the advice he repeated in his *Almanack* against the dangers of wealth: "He does not possess wealth, it possesses him"; "Poverty wants some things, luxury many things, avarice all things"; and "Avarice and Happiness never saw each other. How then should they become acquainted." Franklin retired from his printing business at the age of forty-two and devoted the second half of his life to public-spirited leisure. Upon retiring, he wrote to his mother: "I would rather have it said, *He lived usefully*, than, *He died rich*."[20] And Franklin did live usefully and famously. Perhaps his frugality writings even won acceptance in part because his use of leisure time in science and politics brought fame and name recognition for his advice on how to prosper in a market economy.

Franklin's *Way to Wealth* achieved popularity in the Western world at a time when England had eclipsed the Netherlands as the center of the world economy. London emerged the new center of world trade, and the British became a prosperous nation of shopkeepers with the highest per capita income in the world. The new British capitalism lacked a persuasive general explanation, a philosophy for highbrows, however, until Adam Smith drew together writings on trade, money, national income, and government policy in his *Wealth of Nations* (1776), which created a general explanation of the workings of the market system. The Scottish professor created the new intellectual field of economics (called political economy at the time), which could be optimistic about greed, capitalism, and the individual pursuit of self-interest because Smith assumed the mechanism of the free market restrained men, made them gentle, and polished and softened their barbarian ways. Not only were men checked by competition, they also shared an inner censor of benevolent traits—frugality, justice, and propriety. These ethical traits insured good conduct which, with the added discipline of the market, glued society together. The natural as well as the moral world operated for beneficial results: occasional prodigals might beggar themselves and impoverish their country, feeding the idle with the bread of the industrious, but these bad citizens could never outnumber public benefactors who saved their money, thus increasing wealth for use in productive employment. Smith believed the moral virtue of frugality predominated over prodigality. "The passion for present enjoyment," he wrote, "though sometimes violent and very difficult to be restrained, is in general only momentary and occasional. But the principle which prompts to save, is the desire of bettering our condition, a desire which, though generally calm and dispassionate, comes to us from the womb, and never leaves us till we go to the grave."[21]

Adam Smith's wonderful world of capitalism assumed that economic growth started with the virtue of frugality. "Parsimony, and not industry," he wrote, "is the immediate cause of the increase of capital."[22] The concept of thrift was so centrally important that Smith did not devote much space to it in his *Wealth of Nations*. The professor surely believed that what he had observed among his frugal Scottish and British countrymen were universal human traits. If frugality and thrift were generically human, or at least British, then the science of political economy need not devote attention to these fixed values. Smith and other economists instead devoted their attention to interferences with the free market. They left sermonizing on the virtues of frugality and thrift to ethical moralizers such as Benjamin Franklin.

Although thrift seemed universal to optimistic Enlightenment observers such as Adam Smith, there were plenty of pessimists in British America who had never believed that progress was inevitable and worried instead over the deterioration of traditional ethics in a commercial society. Christians in British America never ceased to worry about weak and profligate human nature. Even secular politicians preached restraint and condemned pleasure. Rhetoric from the Protestant ethic so pervaded the culture that even the American War of Independence became a struggle of frugal, industrious, and virtuous Americans against assaults of a corrupt mother country debased by luxury, extravagance, and vice. Wealth and prodigality had debauched the mother country just as they had earlier corrupted Rome. If Americans were to preserve their liberties, patriots declared, they must practice the virtues of frugality, thrift, and industry. Boycotting British consumer goods combined patriotism and frugality. SAVE YOUR MONEY AND YOU WILL SAVE YOUR COUNTRY, the patriot press proclaimed.[23]

Even formerly profligate Southern planters were now proclaiming peasant values. Tobacco planters had lived in a spendthrift culture. The profligate elite, who had spent too heavily for big houses, fast horses, and sumptuous finery, had plunged deeply into debt to British merchants. Fear of bankruptcy on the eve of the American Revolution, however, drove the Southern gentry to reaffirm traditional thrift. Planters embraced frugality and nonimportation as means of preserving honor and resisting British court and creditors. In proclaiming rural virtue against commercial and royal corruption, revolutionary planters spoke in the tradition of Roman republican and British country moralists.[24]

The lamp of Roman experience was so much a part of popular culture that even George Washington's soldiers performed Addison's *Cato*, dramatically contrasting the rural virtue of thrifty Cato with the ambition, vice, and prodigality of Caesar. In the closing lines of the play, the moral hero advised his sons to abandon corrupt urban civilization for rural virtue, to flee back to the Sabine fields "where the great Censor toiled with his own hands, and all our frugal ancestors were blest in humble virtues and a rural life."[25]

The American republic emerged amidst feverish declarations of frugality, thrift, and public virtue. Popular histories of classical republics insisted that this form of government survived only as long as citizens practiced the self-restraining virtues. The life cycle of governments always descended, it was said, when citizens gave in to prodigality and licentiousness and abandoned the restraint on which republics were built. According to the patriots, American freedom required that the vices of immorality and prodigality be suppressed and the individual virtues encouraged. Even after winning independence, Americans worried that citizens were exchanging prudence, industry, and economy for those glaring vices of luxury, prodigality, and profligacy.[26]

Rhetoric of thrift pervaded discussions in the American republic for the next century. In a formative moment, consumption, display, and extravagance had been pronounced un-American, and the reverse had been elevated to patriotic. Virtuous thrift, to be sure, meant different things to different people. Freehold farm families understood peasant parsimony to be patriotic. Town merchants preferred thrift to mean the capital-

ist's prudent management of money. But all agreed that traditional thrift implied restraint on consumption—a moral quality
in constant danger of decline. Seeking to preserve frugality and
restraint in their republic, worried leaders moralized in all the
peasant, religious, and capitalist traditions.

2

Habits Instilled by the Church

In 1831, Alexis de Tocqueville observed that Americans were unique in their democracy, evangelical Protestantism, and love of money. "Love of money," he wrote, "is either the chief or a secondary motive at the bottom of everything the Americans do." This passion for money represented the opposite of religious conviction for Tocqueville, who believed that all religion lifts human thought above worldly riches. And yet, evangelical Christianity seemed to have an exceptional grip on Americans, reigning "supreme in the souls of the women" who shaped the mores or "the habits of the heart." American men also believed in the Christian heaven—or pretended to—because they controlled their passions, sacrificing pleasures of the moment to win heavenly happiness in the next world. Typical Americans appeared to love both religion and dollars.[1]

A little reading in the works of Protestant leaders could have eliminated the contradiction in American character which puzzled Tocqueville. But he would, of course, have had no assistance from Max Weber's *The Protestant Ethic and the Spirit of Capitalism* (1905), which would later explore the relationship between religion and capitalism. Weber surely exaggerated in saying that Protestantism created the rational spirit of capitalism.

Systematic profit making was much older, but Weber clearly explained Protestant encouragement for industry and frugality. He exposed the psychological sanctions by which Protestantism promoted capital formation.[2]

Max Weber built his case for a new Protestant personality on the observation that John Calvin's theology created great insecurity about individual chances for salvation from the fires of hell. Believers were terrorized by the fear that God had predestined virtually all humans to the horrors of eternal punishment. No priests, no sacraments, no Roman Catholic magic could save the doomed individual. The psychological crisis resulting from fear of this inevitable destiny—a destiny in which man could do nothing to win his salvation—strangely resulted in believers acting as if they were the elected, in hopes that they really were. If Calvinists believed that man was placed on earth to glorify God rather than to indulge himself, then believers practiced industry, sobriety, and frugality in their brief pilgrimage through this world to the next. The psychological consequence of a pessimistic Calvinism, according to Weber, was a fanatical concern with everyday conduct.[3]

English Puritans agreed with Calvin that Christianity required frugality. William Ames reasoned that if wealth came from God, to be held in trust by man, then the eighth commandment—Thou shalt not steal—required parsimony. One holding God's wealth in trust must manage the funds as a faithful servant, using the money to glorify God. Any money spent for pleasure, luxury, or sport stole from God. Christian frugality required "that wee do not lay out our money upon vaine, and unprofitable things."[4] The Protestant ethic did indeed create a religious compulsion to save, helping to accumulate capital in Protestant lands.

The Calvinists and Puritans, of course, did not officially endorse capitalism. Businessmen whose appetites craved profit without end were guilty of "covetousness," while those who practiced economic individualism were said to be under the sin of "greed."[5] Sin flowed inevitably from an ungodly love of money. A fundamental maxim of Christian social ethics had been the words of St. Paul to Timothy: "Having food and raiment, let us be therewith content. For the love of money is the root of all evil." And Jesus himself preached in his Sermon on the

Mount (Matthew 6:19–21): "Lay not up for yourselves treasures upon Earth, where moth and rust doth corrupt, and where thieves break through and steal: But lay up for yourselves treasures in heaven, where neither moth nor rust doth corrupt and where thieves do not break through and steal: For where your treasure is, there will your heart be also."

In theory, the souls of the proud and the covetous were officially assigned by Puritans to hell, but in practice those amassing profits for themselves were difficult to distinguish from those laboring for God. Reverend Cotton Mather's advice on diligence could be as useful to a secular capitalist as to a Christian:

I tell you with *Diligence* a man may do marvellous things. *Young* man, *Work hard* while you are *Young*: You'll Reap the Effects of it, when you are *old*. Yea, How can you ordinarily Enjoy any Rest at *Night* if you have not been well at *Work*, in the *Day*? Let your *Business* Engross the *most* of your Time. Tis not now and then an Hour at your *Business* that will do. Be stirring about your *Business* as Early as tis Convenient. Keep close to your *Business*.

Mather was equally insistent on frugality.

Take this advice, O Christian; Tis a *Sin*, I say, 'Tis Ordinarily a *Sin*, and it will at Length be a shame, for a man to *Spend* more than he Gets, or make his *Layings out* more than his *Comings in*. A frequent Inspection into the *State of your Business*, is therefore not among the least *Rules of Discretion*. It was among the Maxims given of old, *Be Thou Dilligent for to know the State of thy Flocks*; That is to say, often Examine the condition of thy Business, to see whether thou go forward or backward, and Learn to Order thy concerns accordingly.[6]

No scholar would argue that Reverend Mather or any other Puritan sought to promote capitalism; nevertheless, their ethical teachings promoted economic activity. The tension between diligent striving for profit and avoiding sinful greed always existed. Consider the 1636 trial of Boston merchant Robert Keayne on the charge of "covetousness." Keayne's profits of more than fifty percent on imported wares resulted in his trial by the Massachusetts General Court and the Boston Church for extorting more than the "just price," taking advantage of his neighbor's need, and pursuing riches rather than Godly glory. Convicted by state and church, Keayne publicly "did with tears, acknowledge and bewail his covetous and corrupt heart," but he privately persisted in believing that his industry, frugality, and wealth were all evidences of a Godly life. The difficulty of pursuing wealth while avoiding worldliness may have led the New England Puritans into a ritualized self-accusation, the Jeremiad, denouncing themselves for lapsing from pious industry into sinful greed.[7]

The Protestant crusade against greedy individualism could produce hypocrisy. Ministers complained of obvious sinners in their congregations who excused avarice and covetousness. "They will plead in defense of a worldly covetous spirit," pastors said, "under the colour of specious pretense of Prudence, Diligence, Frugality, Necessity."[8] These virtues could easily be practiced for selfish ends, and ministers discovered the difficulty of restraining the thrifty from drifting over the line from religious to secular ethics.

The new Protestant temperament thrived in the North American colonies, where Puritan emphasis on self-mastery built an effective conscience—a superego—that channeled human drives into religion, work, and saving. Philip Greven has explained that evangelical Protestant parents broke their children's will and their determination to resist domination, even starved them into submission so that the children might then more easily submit to God. This evangelical war against the individual self, the appetites, inculcated the self-denial required of Christians, that inner conscience which restrained appetites in sex, dress, diet, and luxury.[9]

The new Protestant temperament characterized not only the Calvinist denominations (Congregationalists and Presbyterians) but also Baptists and the new, eighteenth-century Methodists whose founder, John Wesley, wrote very specifically on child rearing as well as frugality and wealth. Wesley has been a favorite of social historians, from Max Weber to E. P. Thompson, providing evidence of the transformation of poor peasants and workers into a disciplined labor force stripped of idleness, sloth, and improvidence. Wesley is said to have shaped the poor into methodical, disciplined, and repressed Christians distinguished by their manners, dress, and gravity of speech. Any backsliding Methodist was expelled for levity, profanity, or lax attendance at the weekly class meetings where the believers watched over each other's moral behavior. In fact, these weekly class meetings were essential for Max Weber's inclusion of Methodists and Baptists in the Protestant ethic. Neither of these sects accepted Calvin's predestination; they believed heaven open to all who sought it. Why, then, were they so terrified about their daily lives? Each had to prove his salvation not to God but to fellow sectarians who judged one's daily life every Wednesday evening. Among Baptists and Methodists, fear of fellow sectarians substituted for fear of predestination.[10]

According to E. P. Thompson, the name *Methodist* emphasized a husbandry of time. Wesley rose at 4 A.M. and sermonized that others had the duty of early rising. "See that ye walk circumspectly," he wrote, "redeeming the time; saving all the time you can for the best purposes; buying up every fleeting moment out of the hands of sin and Satan, out of the hands of sloth, ease, pleasure. . . . " This new insistence on thrift of minutes led to the teaching of time as money which distinguished the English industrial workers of the 1830s by their greater regularity and methodical repression of leisure.[11]

The poor willingly submitted themselves to what E. P. Thompson denounced as a pitiless ideology of work because Methodism promised something in return—a caring community of believers and hope in this and the next world. Unlike Calvinism, Methodism offered a democratic heaven with gates opened wide for all. Surely the religion should not be viewed as crushing the spirit of the proletariat, as E. P. Thompson charged, but as raising worker hopes with a message of liberty and equality for all who embraced Christian perfectionism and drove sin from their hearts. Was it repression for Wesley to exhort his societies "to avoid sloth, prodigality, and sluttishness," to be clean and neat, to "mend your clothes, or I shall never expect you to mend your lives," to "let none every see a ragged Methodist," to drink no alcohol, "touch no dram," to "lose no time," to "never leave anything till to-morrow, which you can do to-day"?[12] Should such exhortations be viewed as repressions, or as survival skills which brought success and pride to those who mastered them?

Wesley frankly preached that men should seek money. "Gain all you can," he urged in his sermon *The Use of Money*. Of course, he added the qualification that gain must not hurt life, health, morality, or neighbors. Pawnshops, taverns, and theaters were prohibited avenues of profit for Methodists. Once a believer had gained money, Wesley's next rule was to "save all you can." He opposed all spending except for bare essentials: "Expend no part of it merely to gratify the desire of the flesh, the desire of the eye, or the pride of life." More specifically: "Waste no part of it in curiously adorning your houses; in superfluous or expensive furniture; in costly pictures, painting, gilding, books; in elegant rather than useful gardens."[13]

After gaining and saving all the money they could, Methodists were instructed to give all their wealth away because riches made it difficult to be a Christian. "Give all you can," Wesley told them. "Render unto God, not a tenth, not a third, not half, but all that is God's, be it more or less." Riches were the trap that Satan had laid for industrious Christians, making them love money, pleasure, ease, and luxury. Wealth was so dangerous a threat to the soul that it should be given away. So while Wesley considered the virtues of industry and frugality and thrift godly, he insisted that the resulting wealth not be retained or it would surely corrupt human character:

I fear, wherever riches have increased, the essence of religion has decreased in the same proportion. Therefore I do not see how it is possible, in the nature of things, for any revival of true religion to continue long. For religion must produce both industry and frugality, and these cannot but produce riches. But as riches increase, so will pride, anger, and love of the world in all its branches. How then is it possible that Methodism, that is, a religion of the heart, though it flourishes now as a green bay tree, should continue in this state? For the Methodists in every place grow diligent and frugal; consequently they increase in goods. Hence they proportionately increase in pride, in anger, in the desire of the flesh, the desire of the eyes, and the pride of life. So, although the form of religion remains, the spirit is swiftly vanishing away.[14]

In 1776, Methodism was the smallest sect in America, with only five thousand believers. By the time of the American Civil

War, however, the denomination—with its circuit-riding ministers and lay class leaders—had become the largest in the United States. The denomination's early teachings of frugality and thrift continued in its *Methodist Magazine*,[15] but frugality references were so infrequent in the official publication that more persuasive evidence of the power of Methodist frugality can be found in the new social history of the American working class.

In Baltimore, the history of Methodism was one of rapid growth. By 1815, seven percent of the city's residents were Methodists. Successful mechanics were especially drawn to the Methodist creed of industry, discipline, and thrift by which skilled workingmen could separate themselves from the lower-class subculture where drinking, gambling, and casual labor predominated. A master mechanic who had experienced the discipline of a seven-year apprenticeship, had lived frugally as a journeyman, and had finally opened his own shop and married at the age of thirty might understandably wish to separate himself from men who devoted their spare time to tippling houses and grog shops. Typical Methodist class leaders were prosperous mechanics who owned an average of $1,247 in property, whereas ordinary property-holding mechanics had less than half as much. These prosperous class leaders held the weekly meetings, and watched over the religious faith and personal behavior of their little groups of believers. They condemned intemperance, ostentatious dressing, gambling, and fighting. Class members surely agreed with the ethics of frugality and enterprise, for they were typically master shoemakers who operated their own shops and employed a few apprentices and journeymen.[16]

In Massachusetts, where shoemaking became the most important source of industrial employment, Methodism and the new factory morality worked together. The shoemaking town of Lynn became the first in New England to welcome Methodism when a local manufacturer invited revivalist Jesse Lee to preach in 1790. This event motivated 108 members of the Congregational parish—where theology offered salvation for few and damnation for many—to withdraw and create a Methodist congregation where all could be saved. As the Methodists became the largest congregation in town, their emphasis on self-discipline, industry, and sobriety was applauded by shoe manufacturers, who sought to replace the old morality of drinking on the job with a new efficiency and self-restraint. There in the local Methodist church in 1826, shoe manufacturers and a handful of clergymen and lawyers organized the Society for the Promotion of Industry, Frugality, and Temperance. This society established institutional supports for the Protestant virtues by creating a savings bank, pushing local prohibition of alcohol, and making poverty odious in the local poorhouse. The new industrial morality found support from Baptists, Quakers, Congregationalists, and Unitarians—so Methodism both led and shared a common Protestant ethic of work and frugality.[17]

While the Lynn experience supports the cultural hegemony interpretation that owners of capital controlled the minds and behavior of the working class, Philadelphia offers an alternative explanation: that industry, frugality, and thrift constituted a genuine working-class culture, one selected by its own members. In Philadelphia, revival Methodism and Presbyterianism had little appeal for the working class until the economic depression of 1837. The chilling effect of hard times and the new appeal of storefront evangelists created fears that the wrath of God had resulted from moral depravity. Religious terrorism frightened thousands of wage earners out of drinking alcohol, playing cards, and loafing on the job. Traditional peasant habits of enjoying drink, leisure, and festivals were abandoned by the 540 Philadelphians who joined the Methodist church (and the almost 900 who joined the Presbyterians) each year. The new evangelical workers joined teetotal clubs and became firm believers in diligence, self-denial, and the individualism that explained poverty as the result of sin and flawed character.

The evangelical, working-class culture separated itself, not without some bigotry, from the old American casual labor—and especially from the new Irish peasant immigrant—and reinforced those values and institutions that reflected the Protestant ethic and promised worldly success. These church members were three times as likely to acquire property as the general Philadelphia population; one-third of the evangelicals owned property. The new Methodists and Presbyterians also experienced occupational mobility: More than half of the journeymen among them had risen to master craftsmen or small retailers by

1850. The internalized work ethic brought measurable worldly success for those Protestant evangelicals in Philadelphia.[18]

To conclude that virtuous workers prospered is not to deny that some self-indulgent Americans succeeded even more handsomely. Consider the wealthy of colonial America, the merchants and planters. Their children were coddled, indulged, and spoiled, according to evangelical observers and historian Philip Greven. Of course, Greven exaggerates in describing an entire category of merchants as indulgent; the evidence reveals instead a class that varied from ascetic Quaker accumulators to flamboyant adventurers. Not the entire colonial merchant class, but only a segment of that class, indulged itself and its children. The opulent style was common among Southern planters, for example. One Virginia gentleman complained that planters spoiled their children because they believed that "to curb their children [was] to curb their genius." Growing up with their wills unconquered, gentry youth frequently devoted their lives to pleasure—eating, dancing, card playing, and outings. Without religious or parental restraint, they became preoccupied with self-display and ornamentation in clothing, food, housing, and style of life. Alcoholism, gambling, and gratification of sexual desire were not uncommon forms of overindulgence in this class where the Church of England inculcated little conscience of self-restraint. But such a self-indulgent class could still prosper without thrift if there were slaves to do work or investments to produce income. Such prosperity among the indulgent continued in the nineteenth century and has been reported by historians intent on disproving social mobility in America.[19]

Although the industrious and frugal did not always become more wealthy than the idle and dissolute, it happened often enough for evangelical ethics to gain dominance over the culture of early nineteenth-century America. Even the rich, Tocqueville observed, were restrained: they did not waste their money on vast palaces and sensual depravity as did European aristocrats. The wealthy in America, inhibited by evangelical religion, thought only of "adding a few acres to one's fields, planting an orchard, enlarging a house, making life even easier and more comfortable . . . and almost without expense."[20] Rich Americans may not have always lived up to Tocqueville's picture of self-restraint, but the French traveler surely captured the dominant cultural belief in industry, sobriety, and thrift as the distinguishing marks of good citizenship.

In the 1830s, Protestant revivalism and the ascetic lifestyle that had been spelled out by Calvin and Wesley gained control of American culture. In the inland cities, the business elite and working class alike converted to the Presbyterian, Methodist, and Baptist revivalism. New support for more rigorous standards of proper behavior forced a decline of more than 50 percent in the per capita consumption of hard liquor during the decade. Evangelical ministers, capitalists, and successful workingmen warred against indulgence in food, housing, clothing, and the workplace. Historians agree that the churches united the dominant culture with the middle-class ethic of self-control and self-discipline; they disagree only about who profited from the habits inculcated.[21]

3

The Frugal Lady

As American women moved from the age of homespun, through the age of fashion, and into the century of the consumer, they carried with them the virtues of their rural, religious past. Even after women moved from the productive farmhouse—with its spinning wheel, weaving loom, poultry, dairy, garden, and soap factory—to the nonproductive city house, they resisted the shift to a profligate consumer mentality. The new urban housewife might lapse in industry and economy, but she could not casually leave the old values behind. She even purchased familiar thrift advice, supporting the most important arbiter of feminine opinion, Sarah Hale. From 1828 until 1878, Hale preached self-restraint, first in Boston's *Ladies' Magazine*, and later in the national *Godey's Lady's Book*.

Old-fashioned biographies praise Sarah Hale for establishing Thanksgiving as a national celebration, writing "Mary had a Little Lamb," and advocating the education of women, while contemporary feminist historians are distressed by her enormously conservative influence in perpetuating separate sex roles.[1] Both ignore her thrift message, even though frugality propaganda was central to her *Keeping House or House Keeping*

(1845), *Boarding Out* (1846), and countless editorials throughout her long career. Hale always insisted that a lady must practice the virtue of frugality if she were to perform her divinely assigned home duties. Frugality and thrift were such traditional values that neither she nor her readers ever thought this aspect of her literary work merited any special praise. Because her frugality messages so accurately mirrored the traditional moral wisdom of the half million women who subscribed to *Godey's Lady's Book*, her writing offers an especially helpful window on the persistence of thrift as a moral value in nineteenth-century female culture.

Hale learned her moral ethics in the New Hampshire backcountry, where she was born in 1788. Her father was a revolutionary war veteran who had sacrificed his health in the struggle for independence and then built a farm in the forest near the village of Newport. Sarah Hale grew up on that farm and in the community Congregational church, where she learned New England puritanism. Taught to read by her mother, Hale acquired higher education from a brother who shared his books while he studied with the local minister and later while he attended Dartmouth College. Hale became a country schoolteacher and then moved to the provincial town of Newport, where she married a young attorney who encouraged both her study and her writing for the local newspaper. Until she was forty, Hale lived outside urban America. Even after moving to Boston, she continued to believe that the country represented virtue while the city stood for corruption. "The country is the strength of our Republic," she would write. "Luxury may enervate our cities . . . but not the country."[2]

After nine happy years of marriage, when Hale was thirty-four, her husband died of pneumonia, leaving her with five children and no money. She attempted sewing and hat making but—preferring writing—she published magazine articles, a book of poems, and then a novel, *Northwood: A Tale of New England* (1827). Inspired by the example of Catherine Sedgwick, the first American woman to publish a popular novel, Hale won surprising fame in this new field for American women.[3]

The two-volume *Northwood* was a morality story. Its hero, Sidney Romelee, was reared by devout, thrifty parents on a New

England farm and then sent for an education and an inheritance to a wealthy but childless relative on a slaveholding South Carolina plantation. The pleasure ethic of Charleston—the race track, billiard table, and theater—overwhelmed Romelee's puritan self-restraint and sapped his character for seventeen years until a visit back to the Northwood family farm, and an accidental loss of his Charleston fortune, allowed the restoration of his New England provincial virtues. Romelee's father told him (and the reader) that life was intended not for pursuit of pleasure and riches, but for devotion to duty and virtue. Only the good could be happy, certainly not those who pursued pleasure. Publication of this celebration of the Protestant ethic brought Hale instant acclaim in New England and an invitation to become the editor of a new woman's magazine in Boston.[4]

The editorship offer came from the Reverend John Blake, and Sarah Hale accepted his call to Boston as "the ordering of Divine Providence."[5] She distributed her children among relatives, except for the youngest infant, and moved to the city. For the next half century, Hale continued to wear the black dress of a widow and to preach a female reform based on her provincial New England Christianity. Her fiction as well as her editorials were written from a literal reading of the Protestant Bible. After later moving to Philadelphia, she continued to regard Christ as central to her message for woman. "In the Gospel of the Lord Jesus is her hope and strength for this world, as surely as for that which is to come," Hale confessed. "She must be pious or she has no power to do good."[6]

In Genesis, God created life from the lowest to the highest forms. Woman was shaped last and, therefore, according to Hale, she was in some sense superior to man. Not in physical strength or intellectual power but in moral superiority, woman was created to assist man. The Old Testament praised those generous women who sacrificed for their sons and husbands. Hannah, Naomi, and Ruth promoted the welfare of those they loved more than their own. For Hale, the most perfect picture of the capable wife was Proverbs 31:10–31.[7]

How hard it is to find a capable wife! She is worth far more than jewels!

Her husband puts his confidence in her, and he will never be poor.

As long as she lives, she does him good and never harm.

She keeps herself busy making wool and linen cloth.

She brings food home from out-of-the-way places, as merchant ships do.

She gets up before daylight to prepare food for her family and to tell her servant girls what to do.

She looks at land and buys it, and with money she has earned she plants a vineyard.

She is a hard worker, strong and industrious.

She knows the value of everything she makes, and works late into the night

She spins her own thread and weaves her own cloth.

She is generous to the poor and needy.

She doesn't worry when it snows, because her family has warm clothing

She makes bedspreads and wears clothes of fine purple linen.

Her husband is well known, one of the leading citizens.

She makes clothes and belts, and sells them to merchants.

She is strong and respected and not afraid of the future.

She speaks with a gentle wisdom.

She is always busy and looks after her family's needs.

Her children show their appreciation, and her husband praises her.

He says, "Many women are good wives, but you are the best of them all."

Charm is deceptive and beauty disappears, but a woman who honors the Lord should be praised.

Give her credit for all she does. She deserves the respect of everyone.

Hale believed that, for a home to be happy, a woman must honor God and her husband by such obedience to family duties. Female industry, frugality, and benevolence were wifely re-quirements which the New England writer sought to teach through her fiction and editorials. Her campaigns against fash-ions of dress, for example, were based on her theological and moral assumptions. If obedience to God's laws defined the good wife, then what good could one say of a woman whose life seemed controlled instead by fashions? If a woman spent her husband's money decorating her figure—if she put "heart, soul, and mind" to the study of fashion—then she wasted assets and time in the pursuit of the caprices of fashion, she lost opportunities of moral and mental improvement, she neglected the education of her children, and she disturbed her husband's peace (if she did not seriously embarrass him by her extravagances).[8]

Sarah Hale began her campaign against fashion by ignoring it. She simply omitted it from her publication. But the demands of the women's market eventually compelled even her literary magazine to exhibit plates of fashion, while she sought to maintain purity by sermonizing: Don't take the dresses too seriously. All American fashion should conform to reason (plain and simple) and religious principle (indulging others, not oneself). "Is it worthy of Christians, " Hale asked, "to spend their best years in studying the form of their apparel? Trifles should not thus engross us, and they need not, if our citizens would only shake off this tyranny of fashion, imposed by the tailors of Paris and London, and establish the national costume."[9]

Hale especially censured wealthy ladies for introducing the love of idle extravagance in dress. Personal display in gauze, muslin, and ribbon impoverished America by leading factory girls to imitate this opulent style of dress, importing the extravagances from Europe and thereby wasting their own and their country's resources. The sin of fashion impoverished both the individual and the nation.[10]

Stylish ladies were even accused of corrupting their own children by teaching them display of wealth which could only lead to superficial, profligate daughters and spendthrift, dandy sons. According to Hale, wealth was a great calamity for character—encouraging avarice, selfishness, ostentation, and debasement. In her first novel, she declared that "this inordinate thirst for riches is the besetting sin of Americans. . . . "Men were generally degraded by the love of money, but women should be above selfish ostentation: "[Woman] must live for others; her happiness must be the reflection of the felicity she dispenses around her." Charity and benevolence should characterize American mothers: "The perfection of human nature is charity; those who labor to make others better and happier are constantly improving their own hearts and minds." Mothers should teach their children not that "time is money" but that "time is the opportunity for doing good."[11] Doing good required simple, frugal examples—helping others to help themselves.

To simply give money to the poor would only weaken their character by teaching dependence rather than the necessary "forethought, industry and economy." Wealthy women should take their Bibles and visit poor women to enlighten, encourage, and aid them. If a poor mother were idle and her children in rags, perhaps the woman needed needles, patches, and thread. If the family had no food, an investigation of the woman's means of purchasing and cooking might prove that the gift of a kettle for making soup would permit more nutritious food to be prepared at less cost. Visits to grocers might locate one who would deal mercifully with poor women who could purchase only in small quantities. "The best charity," Hale wrote, "is that which teaches, aids, and incites the poor to help themselves. In our country there is more suffering among poor women from idleness, ignorance, and wastefulness than from the want of work, or even from the high prices of the articles of living."[12]

Sarah Hale did more than talk self-help benevolence. She personally organized the Seamen's Aid Society in Boston. The poor wives of sailors became a special concern of Hale's, perhaps because one of her own brothers had perished at sea, leaving a widow and children. She led Boston women in conducting a fair, raising a thousand dollars, and then opening a seaman's clothing store that employed 50 widows and paid them more than double the wages they had previously earned from sewing. The society then expanded into a nonprofit lodging house, a trade school for girls, and a free library.[13]

Hale's advocacy of industry, economy, and temperance was never packaged as a means of helping the poor to rise from rags to riches. She specifically objected to Benjamin Franklin's maxims as a way to wealth. "The poor should not be flattered with the hope of getting rich in this way," she wrote, "because not one in a thousand ever will, by common industry, become rich, and they should not be incited to desire it. But they can all live comfortably and happily and respectably if they will be industrious, reasonable and good." Christian women should have a higher aim for improvement than gaining money. "To toil for wealth that we may enjoy it *ourselves* is a vain thing," Hale said, but "to earn and save that we may thereby make *others* happier and better and wiser, that we may do good seems the only rational method of teaching true economy."[14]

To instruct city girls in their domestic duties—skills that rural girls learned in the farm home—Hale published a series on "domestic economy" in 1840, warning that the prospects of family and nation depended upon woman's mastery of food. "It is usually in the failure of her part alone," Hale said, "that the prospects of her family can be utterly blighted, and the whole happiness of domestic life marred and destroyed. . . . " Every woman, no matter how wealthy, would someday discover that the "comfort and health of her husband and children" depended on her mastery of baking bread. After all, public bakers often resorted to chemical additives and spoiled flour, decent kitchen help could not always be hired, and a husband's financial failure might require one to economize on family expenses. Besides, the half hour spent kneading four loaves of brown bread provided "one of the most beneficial exercises our young ladies could practice. The exercise of the hands and arms, in such a way as to strengthen all the muscles of the body is very seldom practiced by the ladies; and hence much of the debility and languor they undergo." So, by baking for the health and comfort of those she loved, a woman also gave herself that healthy pink glow, as well as soft and beautiful hands.[15]

Sarah Hale's cookbook offered no encouragement for those who regarded culinary skills as consumer arts for pampering friends and gaining a reputation for setting the best table in town. Hale defined cooking as "the art of preserving health, of saving expense, of preventing waste, and of promoting the real and innocent enjoyments of home." Almost every family might keep a good table because a "great variety of relishing dishes, nutritive, and even elegant, may be prepared from the most cheap and common materials." And was it not "a thousand times more important that the bread, necessary to the health and comfort of those we love, and which is required at every meal, should be made in the best manner . . . than that the cake, made for the 'dear five hundred friends,' who attend a fashionable party for their own amusement, sometimes found in ridiculing the hostess, should be 'superb'?"

The possibility of downward mobility for wealthy families was a recurring theme in Hale's editorials. Every extravagant wife married to a businessman ought to keep in mind that her husband might someday be bankrupt. When the financial panic of 1837 brought ruin to many, Hale wrote with apparent satisfaction that the wives of the bankrupt were now freed from the slavery to money. Rejoice, Hale told her readers, for "you are no longer expected to give stylish parties to guests who care not for you, only as you happen to be reputed rich. You need not devote your mornings to idle calls, and your evenings to ceremonial visits. You are relieved from that terrible evil, 'bad help.' " The previously rich were no longer compelled to put up with uncomfortable travel to fashionable resorts but could retreat to the pleasant cottage in the country where children could enjoy healthy outside play and gather strawberries and flowers. The husband could support the family by honorable manual labor, and the wife could be happy doing her duty to encourage and sustain spouse and children.[16]

Sarah Hale condemned the urban extravagance she observed during her first decade of city life. "American ladies—there was never a time . . . since the close of the Revolutionary war, when the practice of true economy was more generally needed," she declared. "The great mass of our people, for the last ten years, have lived beyond their incomes; they have dressed too fine, and each family has aimed at being thought richer than its neighbor." Purchasing on credit was especially condemned as leading to extravagance. Men were, of course, in charge of the credit business, but women should also repent for the encouragement they had given to this extravagance by buying French lace and other foreign "frippery."[17]

Profligate American women so distressed Sarah Hale that she determined to package her frugality message in novel form. Young women were then reading the new domestic novels, and this genre offered the best means of propagandizing them to perform their Christian obligations. In *Housekeeping* (1844) Hale created a frivolous young wife, Mary Harley, whose character had been so damaged by excessive flattery when she was a beautiful young debutante that she continued to think only of superficial charm—beauty, style, and fashion. Even after the indulged girl became a wife and mother, she refused to learn how to boil water or manage servants. She went through thirteen domestics in three years, acquiring enormous bills, poor cooking, dangerous child care, and a home in constant uproar while she pursued the recognitions of society. The crisis developed as Mary made preparations for an extravagant party with 300 guests and drove her husband to fears of financial ruin.[18]

The desperate Mr. Harley turned to his widowed Aunt Ruth, inviting her in from the country to rescue the family from financial chaos that had wasted, in three months, more than enough money to purchase a small farm. The shocked Aunt Ruth observed: "Economy is the order of the universe; no woman should think it beneath her to follow in her household the rule which governs the operations of Providence." But, of course, Mary did think it beneath her to be a "miser," a "drudge," or "plain." Aunt Ruth took high Christian ground: "We are accountable for the use we make of our wealth. . . . Everyone should set apart something for the good of others; besides, we ought to provide for the future, lest, by any accident, we should be rendered incapable of activity and further accumulation." Then Aunt Ruth told Mary an old wives' tale:

I had a neighbor once, who lavished all she could obtain upon herself—dressed richly, and gave splendid entertainments—yet was always excusing herself from visiting the needy, because her time was so fully occupied with her numerous friends. At length her husband failed, and they were obliged to sink into comparative obscurity, deserted entirely by those butterfly friends who had basked in her sunshine.[19]

Mary consented only to permit Aunt Ruth to restore order in the house, but she would not promise to observe and learn management herself. Aunt Ruth fired the three worthless servants and trained new ones to put the whole house back into shape, one room at a time, while Mrs. Harley continued to spend her days and nights in fashionable society. The home became well-regulated, comfortable, and rational under Aunt Ruth's management. Finally, Mrs. Harley weakened before the Christian example and confessed: "Aunt, I begin to feel that there is no pleasure in the kind of life I lead." She repented of self-love, and now devoted to her child and husband the evenings she once frittered away in society. She kept expenses within income, and her husband did not fail as did a few of her society friends'. She developed mental and moral graces which gave her charm in conversation, a social skill in which she had formerly been only superficial. But despite her frugality, she dressed well. "It was acknowledged," Sarah Hale wrote, "even by her fashionable friends that Mrs. Harley dressed with elegant simplicity."[20]

Enlightened simplicity was a dominant theme in the writings and social ethics of Sarah Hale. She wrote in the tradition of those puritan and republican censors who sought to compel their fellow Americans to adopt a life style of "plain living and high thinking."[21] These puritanical republicans had sought to make the American revolution not only a rebellion against monarchy and aristocracy, but also a rejection of decadent, degenerate, self-indulgent European extravagance. Hale's social criticism was in the tradition of the revolutionary Sam Adams's jeremiads against luxury, prodigality, and profligacy. Plain republicans had always hoped to abolish aristocratic practices and establish a republic of virtue in America.

The evils of fashion, vanity, and self-display threatened to create an aristocracy among the wealthy and undermine the finances of less prosperous republicans who were striving for an equal standing in the American democracy. "In our country where every family wishes to appear 'respectable,' " Hale wrote, "it is essential to know how to make the most of small means." Women must practice economy with their needle: "No American woman, let her speak all the tongues, and play all the instruments invented, can be said to be educated if she is not a good needlewoman." Any woman might easily learn to make her own gowns, and, with a little ingenuity, turn and refit them to extend their use. Dress patterns were published in *Godey's*, according to Hale, to encourage "pleasant home enjoyments of winter evenings, when brothers read and the sisters sew, and the family circle is found the center of improvement as well as happiness." Even wealthy women were not exempt from Hale's requirement of needlework: "An extravagant woman can never be an amiable or lovable one. Too often she destroys the comfort of her home, if she does not ruin the fortunes of her husband. Economy is essential in a well-regulated household; no amount of wealth excuses waste, or renders waste attractive."[22]

Frugality, thrift, and efficiency were intended to permit women the time and money to become "God's appointed agent[s] of morality," in and out of the home. Women had the most important work—that of teaching the children. Their duty required "leading the infant mind into the ways of truth and obedience; and giving to childhood habits of diligence, virtue, care of others, self-denial, and that faith in the word of God which will lead them to Christ. . . . " To teach faith and virtue, women had first to study, according to Hale (who was, after all, the literary editor reviewing all books), and not just fiction and the Bible. The education of women was one of her lifelong causes. She applauded every advance in female education and especially campaigned to have women replace men as elementary school teachers. Women, the more moral sex, should be in charge of all the nation's children, both in the home and in the school.[23]

Hale would give women controlling power over their homes, their children, and their social lives, but not the outside world of work and government. Teaching and women's medicine were special situations, but generally God had not designed women to work outside the home or to vote. If women needed legislation to protect their property or to suppress the vices of men that threatened the home, they should use their influence with their husbands and sons. "Let all mothers train up their sons to be good men," she said, "and we should have good legislators who would speedily reform what is now unjust and injurious in our laws. . . . Will a good son consent that his mother—that any mother should be wronged or oppressed?"[24]

Sarah Hale always championed separate spheres for the sexes. "We have no *penchant* for man's work," she wrote in her celebration of distinguished women, *Woman's Record* (1851). "We hold the doctrine that woman's duties are one of a higher and holier nature than man's inasmuch as to her is consigned the *moral power of the world*." To best prepare for her role as a moral influence on men required that a woman have an intellectual education as rigorous as a man's. The only educational difference should be a practical one required by their separate duties. All girls should master "domestic science"—the kitchen, laundry, and sewing room—so that no husband would be forced to suffer an extravagant or ill-run home.[25]

Hale complained that American schools for women were only half-educating young ladies after the Civil War. She applauded the study of arts and sciences for expanding, strengthening, informing, cultivating, and adorning the mind. Women educated purely in arts and sciences, however, were trained only to be princesses. Girls must also be taught the science that made the home "happy and prosperous." Ignorance of household economy left middle-class women "dependent on ill-trained domestics, their homes . . . ill-kept, their husbands . . . displeased, and their children uncomfortable. . . ."[26]

For half a century, Sarah Hale ruled as the American woman's scold—censoring consuming appetites, love of self, and thoughtless extravagance. She could even applaud financial panics because they brought on a proper punishment for a national fault of character—spending all one's income. The depression of 1873, according to Hale, "came just in time to put an end to an era of public and private extravagance, and to bring us back, by a sharp but salutary discipline, to the economy and plainness of living which should distinguish the people of a republic." As America celebrated its first century of independence from Britain, Hale asked: "Will our centennial help to bring us back to the times of republican plainness, and, we may add, of Spartan digestions, when Benjamin Franklin will entertain the magnates of his day with a supper of bread and milk and cucumbers, without forfeiting his good repute as one of the most genial and generous of men?"[27]

When Hale finally ended her public career in December 1877, she wrote: "Having reached my ninetieth year, I must bid farewell to my countrywomen, with the hope that this work of half a century may be blessed to the furtherance of their happiness and usefulness in their Divinely appointed sphere." She had reached beyond her mother's culture by pursuing a literary career and by supporting women's education, and advocating female colleges, teachers, and doctors. She had established the Bunker Hill Monument and the national celebration of Thanksgiving. But she had also kept the faith of her mother's New Hampshire culture by continuing to advocate a traditional benevolent practice of frugality and thrift by women.[28]

4

Savings Banks

"The establishment of savings banks ought to be celebrated as a great event in the world, no less than the introduction of the compass, or the invention of printing," Willard Phillips declared in praise of the new solution to urban poverty. This Boston judge and economist believed that the invention of a thrift institution by his generation could eliminate the problem of urban poverty in the nineteenth century.[1]

All nineteenth-century American discussions of savings banks and the poor were informed by the British example. In Britain, poverty had become a national issue when, in the generation after 1785, the cost of poor relief quadrupled to almost eight million pounds. This distressing poverty actually stemmed from rapid industrial changes aggravated by bad harvests and the trade disruptions of the Napoleonic wars. Contemporary analysts, however, focused their attention not on economic changes, but on Britain's poor laws and Thomas Malthus' *Essay on Population* (1798), which made the melancholy point that population tended to increase faster than the food supply, thereby dooming most of the human race to misery and vice. Malthus, who rejected Adam Smith's optimistic belief that the rising tide of commerce would enrich all, denied any possibility of material progress. By renouncing the earlier generation's enlightened belief in progress, the pessimistic Malthus weakened British support for assisting the poor and promoted instead a view of poor laws as mistaken generosity that only increased the number of unnecessary, improvident paupers.[2]

In frugal Scotland, fear that pauperism might spread north from England led a Dumfrieshire pastor to create a savings bank. The Reverend Henry Duncan's town of 1,100 had no factories or able-bodied paupers. Most of Dumfrieshire's inhabitants were poor but employed cottagers. These rural and small-town Scots were horrified by the subsidized poverty in England, where more than 11 percent of the population was supported by public charity. To avoid such a disaster (and the heavy local taxes to support such welfare payments), Reverend Duncan organized a bank in 1810 and published its plan as *An Essay on the Nature and Advantages of Parish Banks; together with a Corrected Copy of Rules and Regulations of the Parent Institution in Ruthwell and Directions for Conducting the Details of Business, Forms Showing the Methods of Keeping the Accounts* (1815).[3]

Reverend Duncan called his bank a "savings and friendly society," borrowing from a tradition of friendly health insurance societies. Traditionally, these local societies held mandatory monthly tavern meetings at which members contributed to the group treasury and participated in social drinking. In return for contributions, members who remained in good health received nothing beyond communal fellowship and a feeling of common security, but those who became sick received money benefits from the common treasury. Nineteenth-century Protestants argued that these old friendly societies promoted drunkenness and irregular work habits along with their fraternal insurance, but the new banks encouraged virtue without these vices.

Because commercial banks did not accept small depositors, (preferring larger funds from stockholders and big depositors), small savers had been forced to hide cash under mattresses or bury it in cellars where it brought no interest (and might even shrink because women were tempted to spend for dress and men to purchase drinks at the tavern). Far more permanent were savings placed in Duncan's bank, where money could be withdrawn only with the permission of the bank directors. Parson

Duncan and his benevolent directors encouraged virtuous self-denial—restraining the temptation to spend for present indulgences while building future economic independence. So paternalistic were the bank rules that depositors were fined if they failed to deposit a certain sum each year. This paternalism offended Scots, who feared that oppressive rules might hinder the spread of this brightest hope for eliminating poverty, so Parson Duncan's rules were ignored by new banks which modeled themselves instead after the more liberal Edinburgh Savings Bank, which permitted unrestricted deposits and withdrawals.[4]

Savings banks appealed to local Societies for Bettering the Condition of the Poor, which created new savings institutions and produced a propagandistic literature—*A Short Account of the Edinburgh Savings Bank* (1815); George Rose's *Observations on Banks of Savings* (1816); Joseph Hume's *An Account of the Provident Institution* (1816); and William Davis's *Friendly Advice to Industrious and Frugal Persons Recommending Provident Institutions or Savings Banks* (1817). All of these agreed that the only effectual way of assisting the poor was to encourage the moral habits of industry, economy, and sobriety. "It is in their own power," William Davis said of the poor, "by a good moral conduct and habits of economy, to avoid the degradation of receiving Parish relief and to raise themselves to a respectable rank, in the scale of society." Working people were assumed to be industrious but ignorant of the necessity of habitually saving small sums. "Saving is as necessary to be taught as reading or writing," Davis said, "for it would be absurd to suppose that Economy is an intuitive faculty of the mind." Just as schools and Bible societies taught literacy and religion, so the new thrift institutions could assist the industrious in depositing small sums and avoiding ale houses, chewing tobacco, and debt while developing a taste for prosperity and virtue. Small savings could indeed lead to riches. Any young, rural laborer could save a reasonable competence of eighty pounds by the age of twenty-five, a young woman twenty to thirty pounds, and a London artisan perhaps two hundred pounds. Savings banks so encouraged the virtue of frugality and thrift that they were said to assist the young in avoiding early marriage, pride of dress, and other personal vices which had produced poor laws and pauperism.[5]

British reform ideas were common throughout the Atlantic world, shared especially by American merchants in the port cities of Boston, New York, and Philadelphia. Protestants were united in their belief in Christian benevolence, their alarm at rising poor rates, and their conviction that individual morality could solve social problems. In December 1816, a Boston religious monthly announced that a local committee of gentlemen had asked the Massachusetts legislature to incorporate a savings bank similar to those in England and Scotland. The editor of Boston's *Christian Disciple* supported the benevolent purpose, writing: "It is not by the alms of the wealthy, that the good of the lower class can be generally promoted. By such donations, encouragement is far oftener given to idleness and hypocrisy, than aid to suffering worth. He is the most effective benefactor to the poor, who encourages them in habits of industry, sobriety and frugality."[6]

Boston organizers of the Provident Institution for Savings regarded their work as Christian charity; they intended to manage this financial institution without salary or benefit to themselves. The benevolent organizers were pleased that their early depositors included "humble journeymen, coachmen, chambermaids, and all kinds of domestic servants, and inferior artisans" who sought a secure bank for their little earnings which might otherwise be squandered or unwisely lent to fraudulent dealers, neighbors, and relatives. The Provident promised not only security for savings but a minimum of four percent interest which could multiply a quarter saved each week into $157.81 in ten years. Among the early depositors, 71 percent were women and children. The female depositors were largely single women and widows, but 62 married women also made deposits. Among the male depositors, some were middle-class merchants, traders, and lawyers, but many more were mechanics and laborers. The Provident trustees refused large deposits because they did not intend to personally profit, but rather to do unpaid work that would morally elevate the poor and encourage temperance, frugality, thrift, and foresight.[7]

Benevolence moved the founders of New York City's saving bank to imitate Boston and Edinburgh. A handful of pious Quakers and Calvinists who were active in local relief organizations organized to lobby for a thrift institution in 1816. Their English inspiration is well-documented. Quaker Thomas Eddy wrote London reformer Patrick Colquhoun, saying: "Among the many philanthropic institutions which your country abounds, there is none that appears to me more likely to be useful than Savings Banks. They are certainly most admirably calculated to be beneficial to the poor by promoting among them a spirit of independence, economy and industry. Immediately on receiving from thee an account of the Provident Institution in your metropolis, I proposed to a number of my friends to establish a similar one in this city."[8]

When early efforts of the Eddy group were blocked by an anti-bank sentiment in the state legislature, the Christian reformers organized a New York Society for the Prevention of Pauperism and published a propaganda report on the causes of poverty. Their 1818 report found the causes of pauperism to be alcohol, idleness, extravagance, early marriage, gambling, pawnbrokers, prostitution, and charitable institutions which rewarded laziness. The report concluded: "Prodigality . . . prevails to a great extent among the poor, it prevails to a great extent in inattention to those small but frequent savings when labor is plentiful. . . . "[9] The cures for "want of economy" were, of course, a savings bank and legislation against alcohol and lotteries.

A second annual report from the society in 1819 included glowing propaganda from the savings banks in Boston, Salem, Philadelphia, and Baltimore and declared savings institutions the best means of decreasing pauperism. How thrilling for reformers to read the Baltimore bank letter: "We have an Irishman, a hard-working stonemason, who has deposited 400 dollars, at different times. Several free blacks, have, from time to time, deposited 100 dollars, and more. We have several instances of women, who, during the whole summer, deposited a dollar per week. This is the most desirable kind of depositor for all this is saved from luxury and dress. Several journeymen mechanics deposit their 3 to 5 dollars per week."[10] Enthusiastic support from the savings institutions forced the legislature to capitulate to the New York Society for the Prevention of Pauperism and approve their request for a savings bank charter in 1819.

Although reformers used benevolent Christian rhetoric as well as the self-interest of reducing the pauper tax to explain their motives, Marxist historians reject the sincerity of such explanations. The real purpose of middle-class reformers, Marxists contend, was to gain power over working-class society for the conservative ends of lower taxes and a docile, brainwashed laboring class.[11] Were the poor brainwashed to use savings banks against their own interests? Did the rapid multiplication of savings banks from 278 in 1862 to 674 (with $850 million saved by two million depositors) in 1875 represent the triumph of middle-class over working-class interests? There is no simple answer to this question because an earlier generation's motives can only be inferred, never proven. Before rejecting that generation's explanation, however, the logic and evidence known to them should be considered. What did political economists, professors, and merchant reformers of the 1820s believe to be true of their economic world?

Boston economist Willard Phillips assumed American poverty to be a recent urban problem in the 1820s. According to Phillips, the earlier American had been a frugal, self-sufficient farmer who was his own carpenter, blacksmith, shoemaker, and mason. With his wife and family, this farmer manufactured or bartered for all household necessities. In the pioneer past, young men had acquired wild tracts of land in exchange for two or three years of agricultural wages and then devoted a few hard years in a log cabin to clearing land and planting corn. As the pioneer and his neighbors subdued the wilderness, their land grew in value. The farm was actually the pioneer's savings bank to which he annually contributed his labor. Away from any populated community, the pioneer easily practiced temperance and frugality because temptations were largely absent. Frugal habits were thus forced on the whole pioneer population and then passed along from generation to generation. Traditional frugality won the support of religion and the writings of Ben Franklin. But the new urban workers needed more incentive, and the savings banks with their compound interest promised to turn laborers into saving capitalists.[12]

Economist Thomas Cooper agreed that there need be no poor in America. This Oxford-educated son of an English manufacturer became a Jeffersonian Republican and taught his South

Carolina students that, while the poor on the American frontier in Illinois were too few to be noticed, Massachusetts counted one pauper in every 68 citizens. Eastern cities were on the road to British pauperism, and the causes were urban idleness, extravagance, dissipation, drunkenness, and vice. Gambling lotteries, dram shops, tippling houses, and poor laws created urban poverty. By eliminating poorhouses for the able-bodied and encouraging savings banks, pauperism would disappear except in truly incapacitated persons. "In this country," Cooper said, "there is no man so poor as not to be able to invest a small weekly sum in an institution of this kind. In ninety-nine out of a hundred instances, this would take away the necessity of a resort to the alms house." If America promoted savings banks, "the habit of temperance, of saving and self denial which they are calculated to introduce, would gradually bring on a tone of moral feeling among the lower classes of society, of incalculable benefit not to them merely, but to the whole community."[13]

Thomas Cooper promoted savings banks from a secular, anticlerical perspective, believing that "the greatest good of the greatest number" established the rationale for social policy. Cooper's utilitarianism was unacceptable, however, to the Christian colleges where most political economy was taught. These schools chose instead to use a text written by Baptist minister and Brown College president Francis Wayland. *The Elements of Political Economy* (1837) found truth in the Bible and quoted the Sermon on the Mount to justify benevolence. Reverend Wayland's Bible, however, compelled benevolence only to assist the aged, sick, disabled, and orphaned—not the poor. The language of revelation—"If a man will not work, neither shall he eat" (II Thess. 3:10)—and reason (poor laws had multiplied poverty in England) persuaded Wayland that only people unable to help themselves should be objects of charity. Poor laws, he insisted, multiplied paupers, vagrants, and idlers when the regulations failed to establish workhouses and compel the able-bodied to work. He believed as firmly in punishing vice and encouraging virtue as any other Calvinist.[14]

The exception to the Anglo-American creed of self-restraint came from Philadelphia, where the Irish-American Mathew Carey spoke the language of manufacturers applauding government tariff protection and consumer spending. The Carey school message was voiced by Daniel Raymond in *The Elements of Political Economy* (1823), which accused excessive thrift of spreading misery and starvation among laboring classes. Raymond attributed manufacturing distress after 1815 to underconsumption resulting from "disgusting" avarice and parsimony.[15]

Despite Raymond, middle-class belief in individual frugality had hardened into a fixed creed much more intense than the half-serious aphorisms of Poor Richard, who wrote for the more traditional world where the customs of aristocracy, paternalism, and state religion prevailed. In the new world of freedom from inherited institutions—where the American was free in politics, economics, and religion—opinion makers naturally responded to the rise of urban pauperism by promoting individual responsibility for industry, frugality, and thrift. American democracy celebrated individualism against the paternalism of Europe.

All observers agreed that city people suffered more poverty and disease than country people. Sickness and disease were far worse in cities, and death rates were twice those of the country until the twentieth century. Before the discovery of germs and their relationship to disease, city people were defenseless against the water- and airborne germs that thrived on urban congestion with its foul water, air, and food. The plague of Asiatic cholera as well as normal disease contributed enormously to city poverty. The connections between human sickness and the developing business cycle of boom and bust as secular causes for urban poverty may be clear to moderns, but they were not to an age that did not understand germs and did not assume the human capacity for controlling business cycles. Americans in the Age of Democracy emphasized what they believed—that city people were more improvident and less thrifty than country people.[16]

If Americans persisted in deserting healthy, country living for the unsafe city life, it was said, then they must resurrect some of the lifestyles of their forefathers. Even the extreme vegetarian diet reform of Reverend Sylvester Graham shared a certain rural fundamentalism with the savings bank movement. City dwellers had abandoned the cornbread and bland vegetable diet of pioneers for refined food, alcohol, tobacco, and other urban excesses—only to succumb to cholera. By returning to a pioneer diet, Graham preached, Americans might recover the healthy life. By returning to country frugality (with the addition of regular thrift deposits), the savings bank reformers argued, urban Americans might recover the economically secure life.

Thrifty factory workers were found in American cities. The Swedish traveler Carl Arfwedson expressed amazement at the 280 gun-factory workers he observed in Springfield, Massachusetts. He witnessed workers who owned three-room homes and raised food in their own fruit and vegetable gardens. "Poverty is seldom discovered among them," he wrote. And why were these American laborers so frugal and hardworking? According to Arfwedson: "First, Temperance Societies, and second, Savings Banks, two establishments which both here and in other manufacturing towns in America have really done wonders among the labouring classes."[17]

Sober Springfield workers were clearly not representative of all laborers in emerging metropolises. In the port cities, immigration doubled the number of paupers. Associations for the improvement of the condition of the poor recognized the problems of unemployment, low wages, sickness, and bereavement, but thought that inculcation of prudential habits—industry, frugality, and temperance—were the main remedies for idleness and vice. Sending workers out to agricultural land was a solution often suggested by anti-urban reformers, but for paupers who remained in the city, middle-class reformers believed that the only cures were evangelical religion and savings banks. Religion, it was said, could lift a worker out of idleness and corruption into moral improvement and virtue. Then the worker would be able to take advantage of the savings banks which had "alleviated more misery, and produced more comfort and morality, than any of the charitable institutions of the land." By regular deposits in the bank, it was said, "the laboring classes soon learn the value of money, and also are led to become more frugal and diligent, to esteem more highly the institutions of society, and to acquire an increased degree of personal worth and moral elevation."[18]

The savings bank became a universal middle-class recipe for prosperity, touted not only by preachers and reformers but also by the fiction of the period. In the pages of *Hunt's Merchant*

Magazine, Oliver Optic developed a short story around the character of an improvident clerk who lived up to the limit of his $888 a year salary until his wife, the daughter of a frugal farmer, gave him a circular from the People's Savings Bank. The circular demonstrated that, with the bank's five percent interest, saving $50 every three months would amount to $1141.25 in five years—enough to build a comfortable house. Charles Converse hadn't saved a dollar until then, spending all his surplus for travel, opera, four-cent cigars, sherry cobblers, ice creams, and three evening papers. His wife observed: "The rain falls in drops but washes the whole earth. Four cents a day, for a year, amounts to about twelve dollars." After Charles figured that his little vices amounted to $268 a year, the idea of saving took possession of him. In only four years, the family built a house and paid for its furniture as well. Through his wife's influence, Charles had been converted to frugality and "resolved to be prudent, economical, saving, even parsimonious."[19]

The best-known social mobility novel of the age was Horatio Alger Jr.'s *Ragged Dick* (1868), in which a poor street boy rose to a middle-class job only a year after receiving advice to be frugal and master the fundamentals of education. Ragged Dick opened a savings bank account and grew in independence, sense of importance, and generous benevolence as he reaped the advantages of his new self-denial and judicious economy, which included giving up subsidizing cigars, the old Bowery, and saloons such as Tony Pastor's. Even without the stroke of luck that landed him a good job at Rockwell's countinghouse, Dick Hunter's savings of more than $100 could have financed his move from bootblack to office boy.

The model of Ragged Dick with his savings account was not as artificial as the critics of capitalism have alleged. Dick Hunter did not rise from rags to riches but only to respectability. And savings accounts were indeed common among unskilled laborers. Stephan Thernstrom found that 38 percent of laboring families in Newburyport, Massachusetts had savings accounts in the first decade after the Civil War. A thrifty and temperate laborer could save as much as $1,000—at a time when a house could be purchased for $300. The scoffers who claimed that most accounts were closed after five years ignored the chief reason for accounts, to save money for the lump-sum repayment of home mortgages. Of course, the scoffers were correct in saying that only one-third of working families owned homes at any one time, but it was also true that the working class included young, middle, and older age groups. Although few young workers had homes, the percentage of home ownership rose to 63–78 percent after 20 years of work, and all the foreign-born (mainly Irish) owned property after 30 years. In addition to home ownership, Thernstrom concluded that "the thrifty and temperate laborer might reasonably hope, with luck, to accumulate a few hundred dollars on which to survive old age at a time when pension plans and social security were unknown."[20]

Although banks certainly helped the laboring class, they were no miracle solution for poverty. In 1876, the leading historian of savings institutions conceded that they would never "make the slothful vigilant; the wasteful frugal; the vicious virtuous." In his *History of Savings Banks in the United States* (1876), Emerson Keyes concluded that only the frugal majority had taken advantage of the opportunity to put aside surplus earnings during prosperous years in preparation for the day of adversity. Savings banks could assist only the industrious and virtuous, not those moved by instinct and passion.

The lowered expectations for savings banks partly explains why these institutions never moved out of the Eastern cities. Only one mutual savings bank had opened in the South, one in the Pacific West, and 19 in the Midwest by the twentieth century. The South and West lacked benevolent and prosperous capitalists who regarded mutual savings banks as miracle cures for pauperism. In fact, the reputation of these benevolent institutions had been tarnished in the speculative economic boom of the American Civil War. The number of banks doubled in the decade after 1862, and some of the new banks were chartered by speculators who posed as benefactors but who really intended to control the banks for private ends. They built expensive offices, paid themselves extravagant salaries, and covered expenses by making speculative loans at high rates of interest. Inevitably, the financial crash of 1873 brought down 20 institutions, twice as many as had failed in the first 60 years of American savings banks. To be sure, reformers drafted fresh legislation to regulate savings bank managers and their loans, but moral distinctions in banking had been blurred, and virtually all newly opened savings institutions were commercial enterprises intended to make profits for their stockholders. The West and South had many eager banking capitalists but few benevolent philanthropists. And although the more than 600 benevolent banks in the East remained firmly established, with total assets exceeding $1 billion dollars in the 1880s, over the next generation they would be outnumbered by commercial banks that advertised for savings accounts.[21]

A new variety of savings institution multiplied rapidly after the Civil War. The building and loan, or cooperative bank, was a British import with its origins in a Birmingham pub. English workers who joined the cooperative had met monthly to make contributions to the common treasury, take out building loans, and handle society business. When all members had built homes and repaid their loans, the society could go out of business. For half a century after the institution came to America (the first organized in Pennsylvania in 1831), building and loan cooperatives remained temporary. A charter innovation in the 1880s, however, permitted permanent building associations that offered easy joining and departure. Anyone could open an account or withdraw savings at any time. The new associations handled deposits just as savings banks did, in addition to making home loans. While savings banks were reluctant to lend more than half their assets on housing, preferring the ease and safety of government or railroad securities, building associations invested all their assets in housing loans and won national popularity, attracting seven percent of all personal savings by the end of the century.[22]

The truly popular form of savings among the urban working class became life insurance. The self-respect of poor laborers required that they have a decent funeral. The American working class, like that of England, willingly sacrificed every week by taking money from current consumption to prepare for the future and avoid the disgrace of a pauper burial. Initially, workers joined fraternal groups for their burial insurance, but by the 1870s private insurance firms were offering them nickel, dime, and quarter policies collected weekly by company agents. These industrial agents sold the status of having a guaranteed stylish burial. We cannot be sure whether individual pride and ego of the worker or the skill of the sales agent was more powerful, but 80 percent of native white families and more than 90 percent of immigrant and black families in industrial towns were insured. Middle-class financial experts were inclined to scoff at the high cost of this industrial insurance, but the laboring classes were apparently more concerned with respectability than large bank accounts. Typical families desired security and respect within their class more than upward mobility into the capitalist class. The life insurance share of personal savings surpassed that of mutual savings holdings in 1915, with 34.6 percent of the American total and an even larger share of working-class savings.[23]

The percentage of workers holding savings accounts was never reported, and families refused to tell outsiders, so mill town investigators could only guess that about half the laboring class had savings accounts. Mugwump economists were certain that widespread and growing savings were reducing poverty. David A. Wells, in *Recent Economic Changes* (1890), reported that pauperism as a percentage of the population was generally decreasing. Deposits held by U.S. savings banks totaled $1.5 billion in 1885, double the amount of a decade before. William Graham Sumner's *History of Banking* (1896) credited the thrift institutions with sponsoring both moral and material growth. According to Sumner, saving tended to "increase the moral perception of the individual; education is encouraged; patriotism is promoted; family honor as well as local pride is engendered; commercial enterprise is stimulated." Not only the savers, but their communities prospered: "Their money it is which is . . . loaned . . . on the apartment and tenement houses in which they dwell, the churches they attend, the clubs, business stores and factories, the theatres and places of amusement they frequent. It is largely their money which is loaned to the city on its bonds for the construction of public buildings and docks, the purchase and improvement of public parks, and paving streets."[24]

Mugwump economists were quick to defend savers and their productive loans from the threat of silver inflation in the 1890s. When Democratic-Populist farmers attempted to double their commodity prices and cut their debts in half by increasing the money supply with silver currency, it became the central issue of the presidential election of 1896. The mugwump press published articles titled "Thou Shalt Not Steal" and "Compulsory Dishonesty," warning that widows, orphans, and thrifty workers with savings deposits, building-association certificates, and life insurance would not be the only ones to suffer. If the Democrats succeeded in punishing thrift and self-denial, the wonderful world of savings, investment, and economic prosperity would never return.

Thrift and the "honest" dollar won the 1896 election against free silver. The industrial Northeast and the Midwest rejected inflation and William Jennings Bryan. If the South and West could not have radical economic change or mutual savings banks, they must have a substitute. Postal savings banks had been a philanthropic solution since the 1860s, when Great Britain had encouraged thrift by establishing savings depositories in her post offices. Beginning in 1871, American postmaster generals regularly endorsed the British savings program. Seventeen separate legislative proposals were introduced prior to 1896. Not only establishment philanthropists, but also populist reformers in the Peoples Party, called for postal savings banks. If half the population in the Northeast held thrift accounts but only one in 57 of other Americans did, an absence of secure banking facilities in the South and West seemed the probable explanation. "The widespread extravagance and improvidence among our people is not so much a defect of character," the postmaster general said, "as it is a defect of conditions that surround our people." Postal savings could create more thrifty, contented, and conservative Americans. Postmaster James A. Gary even predicted that "every man who [had] a bank account with the Government, however small, would be less liable to join in mob violence or revolution." The New England-born cotton manufacturer made postal savings the focus of his 1897 annual report, but the objections of commercial bankers delayed until 1910 the establishment of a savings bank in every community with a post office. Meager interest payments of two percent on deposits kept postal banks from becoming major holders of savings—they held only $90 million by 1916—but the government banks did make thrift deposits possible for Westerners and Southerners.[25]

As the 630 mutual savings banks approached their centennial in 1916, they held most thrift deposits in the East, but had permitted profit-making savings banks to take over the propaganda war for thrift. The 1,629 commercial savings banks even directed the public commemoration of a century of savings banking. These members of the American Banking Association, in cooperation with the Young Men's Christian Association, organized a national thrift commemoration. In their propaganda, the commercial savings banks merged their assets with the mutuals and boasted that 2,159 savings banks with ten million depositors held $4.7 billion in deposits. The thrifts held enormous deposits and could boast to the nation that their wonderful moral influence in persuading America to save had resulted in public order, industrial development, and national prosperity. Americans were probably saving 15 percent of their personal income in part because of a century of assistance and encouragement from thrift institutions.[26]

5

Thrift in the Schoolhouse

The common school in America opened without any intent to teach the saving of money: Where thrift is widely practiced, a culture has no need to drill children in adding to their piggy banks. The community preferred a moral nursery that taught children obligations to God and community rather than self. School sponsors wanted no Lockean individualism, no unrestricted self-interest or free satiation of the appetites. They sought instead to inculcate the restraint of Protestant Christianity, which insisted on self-control, virtue, and concern for the community. To repress Lockean individualism, the schoolhouse taught its pupils to fear a stern God who administered justice as well as love—in this world and in a real Heaven and a horrible Hell. The classroom taught concern for others and care for God's community with an intensity that precluded, until after the Civil War, direct instruction in the saving of money.

The early school indifference to capital accumulation reflects the evangelical religious origins of common schools in the early nineteenth century. Once church and state separated in America, old parochial schools could not hope to reach the generation liberated from state religion. In New York City, for example, transition to the new, interdenominational school is well-documented. In 1805, a dozen Protestants organized The Society for Establishing a Free School in the City of New York, for the Education of Such Poor Children as Do Not Belong to or are not Provided For, by Any Religious Society. Within three years, the society had acquired state aid, recruited children, and begun to displace parochial schools (except for Roman Catholic, Dutch Reformed, and Associate Reformed Presbyterian). New York's schools may have been called public and nondenominational, but they continued to teach Protestant religion.[1]

The interdenominational school also triumphed in the American West. New communities were divided among Congregationalists, Episcopalians, Methodists, Baptists, and Presbyterians, but no group was numerous enough to develop a separate denominational school. If a community were to have any school for teaching reading, writing, and arithmetic, a common one shared by all Protestants and supported by parental subscriptions was the best available choice.

In the Ohio Valley, Protestants united to build such a system of public education—one in which religious values were inculcated in the schoolroom.[2] The minds of the school boards and teachers of nineteenth-century middle-American children have been preserved in the textbooks of William Holmes McGuffey, the Presbyterian minister and Miami University professor who developed the most popular school readers. McGuffey's *Eclectic First Reader* (1836) is a God-centered text that permitted learners only 14 pages of John-and-Jane and dog-and-animal stories before beginning serious moral instruction. Children read that God created and watched over their world, that they must be benevolent to poor old beggars, animals, and their fellow creatures. God wanted boys and girls to be studious, kind, obedient, and helpful, and to pray for forgiveness in any wrongdoing. They must not disobey their parents, destroy bird nests, abuse cats, engage in mischief, drink alcohol, overeat, lie, swear, or steal. According to the *First Reader*, "bad boys lie, and swear, and steal," and good children must not play with "boys that speak bad words or tell lies." Shame and guilt embarrassed those who broke the rules, but the good little chimney sweep—who resisted temptation and refused to steal the golden watch because he knew God was watching—found good luck (as opposed to the prison that awaited the thief). Even first graders were to repress bad impulses and strive to do God's will.

The *Second Reader* was even more precise about God's will. Morality tales identified bad characteristics as idleness, greed, cruelty, mischief, malice, ignorance, slovenliness, vanity, anger, envy, theft, disobedience, drunkenness, and profanity. The good virtues were charity, generosity, industriousness, diligence, piety, honesty, character, obedience, temperance, and prayer. The *Second Reader* also included Bible selections—Solomon, and Joseph and the Ten Commandments—but real Bible study began in the *Third Reader*. McGuffey made no apology for extracts from the King James Scriptures. "The time has gone by," he wrote, "when any sensible man will be found to object to the Bible as a school book, in a Christian country, unless it be on purely sectarian principles. . . . "Of course, McGuffey and other evangelicals found nothing sectarian about most Bible verses.

McGuffey included essays written by members of most mainstream Protestant denominations—Congregational, Episcopalian, Presbyterian, Methodist, Baptist, and Unitarian. These essays never touched on sectarian differences, but expressed instead commonly shared beliefs. Unitarian William Channing, for example, offended no evangelicals with his "Religion the only Basis for Society." What Christian believer could object to Channing's argument that the social order of America rested on enlightened piety? Without personal belief in a Supreme Being, Channing wrote, the whole social fabric would rip under the resulting rapacious individualism. "Erase all thought and fear of God from a community, and selfishness and sensuality would absorb the whole man," Channing wrote. And: "Appetite, knowing no restraint . . . would trample in scorn on the restraints of human laws. Virtue, duty, and principle would be mocked and spurned. . . . A sordid self-interest would supplant every feeling, and man would become, in fact, what the theory of atheism declares him to be—*a companion for brutes.*"

Where in this God-centered world of the McGuffey Readers was the habit of saving money? There were no selections from Franklin's "Way to Wealth," and no essay was included for the purpose of promoting saving money. The nearest to an endorsement of savings was an endorsement of laying aside money to pay teachers: "My parents are very good to save some of their money in order that I may learn to read and write." The McGuffey view of money would have pleased early Puritans, Martin Luther, or medieval Catholics. The miser was depicted in the Readers as a hated, disgusting figure who sacrificed all virtues for avarice. Frugality and thrift, on the other hand, were approved Christian virtues if they promoted benevolence. The girl who avoided extravagant dress and saved money to give to the poor found applause in the *Second Reader*. But benevolence— not saving money—was the applauded virtue. In another selection, a Russian peasant, Flor, could have become rich when grain famine offered opportunity to sell corn from his abundant granaries to the famished at high market prices. Instead, Flor freely gave from his abundance and accepted no payment in return. McGuffey applauded not the accumulation of wealth but caring concern for the community.

The Readers had no admiration for wealth. "Is it not better to be industrious and have a good name, than to possess many riches?" the *Second Reader* asks after instructing the poor boy not to envy those who have pretty horses and fine clothes. Remember, "it is God who makes some poor, and others rich—that the rich have many troubles which we know nothing about and that the poor, if they are but good, may be very happy."

While never promoting wealth, neither did McGuffey condemn it. One of his more secular essays promised that individual merit and industry would be rewarded: "The road to wealth, to honor, to usefulness, and happiness, is open to all, and all who will but enter upon it with the almost certain prospect of success. In this free community there are no privileged orders. Every man finds his level. If he has talents, he will be known and estimated. . . . " So McGuffey recognized individual merit, but he would never have repeated Benjamin Franklin's cynical aphorism: "God helps those who help themselves."

The McGuffey school of indifference to capital accumulation probably reflected only the common schools of the rural Ohio Valley before the Civil War. McGuffey Readers never sold in the Northeast, where textbook writers Noah Webster and Peter Parley found Benjamin Franklin's secular individualism perfectly acceptable. Noah Webster had broken with the old theological emphasis on sin, death, and eternal damnation after the American Revolution and published a more worldly *Blue-Back Speller* in 1783. This *Speller* omitted most of the religious material, replacing it with wisdom literature of the Poor Richard style. Secular proverbs were also offered in Webster's *Reader*, including the thrift wisdom:

Without frugality none can be rich, and with it, very few would be poor.

Though in every age there are some, who, by bold adventures or by favorable accidents, rise suddenly into riches; the bulk of mankind must owe their affluence to small and gradual profits, below which their expenses must be resolutely reduced.[3]

The McGuffey Readers represented a rural retreat back to the religious style from which Noah Webster and the Northeast had broken during the revolutionary period. Eventually, commercial development in the Midwest would bring secular demands on the Cincinnati textbook publisher to revise the McGuffey Readers three times and move God from the center. These later editions, in which McGuffey had no editorial participation, were the basis for a more capitalist version of the Readers.[4]

Protestant evangelicalism of the McGuffey style lost out in post-war urban America to Irish-Catholic pressure and the more secular perspective of teachers and intellectuals in a commercial world. Although the struggle to remove religion from the schools would continue for more than a century, early victories occurred in New York City in the 1840s when Bishop John Hughes's campaign for state funding of parochial schools led the common schools to drop devotional use of the Bible. If religion were not preached in the classroom, Irish children might enter the public schools and be Americanized into virtuous voters and workers. Universal education, with or without religion, was now demanded as a preventive measure against pauperism, crime, and corrupt politics. The Presbyterian *Princeton Review* observed in 1865 that "a great city without schools would be a hell;—a seething caldron of vice, impurity and crime." The Protestant nation with the least adequate common schools, England, produced "pauperism . . . an evil which her wisest statesmen have given up as unmanageable." Compulsory schooling, with or without religion, seemed essential for preserving social order. The largest Protestant denominations were willing to let the Bible go from the classroom in hopes of luring Catholics into the common schools.[5]

When the Bible actually did get ejected, as when the 1869 Cincinnati school board resolved "that religious instruction and the reading of religious books, including the Holy Bible, are prohibited in the common schools of Cincinnati," a firestorm of Protestant protest resulted. But secularization won in this city that published the McGuffey Readers. Roman Catholicism, after all, had become the largest denomination there. By the late 1880s, Catholic opposition had also pushed the Protestant Bible out of schools in Chicago, St. Louis, Detroit, Milwaukee, San Francisco, New Orleans, and Atlanta. By the twentieth century, 99 cities prohibited the Bible, but Protestant persistence in 651 smaller cities continued devotional use of the Bible.[6]

Just as devotional Bible reading left the urban schools, so did Protestant theology retreat from school readers. The central reader of the Gilded Age was not that assembled by the Presbyterian minister but the new *Appleton Reader* (1878), produced by William Torrey Harris, St. Louis school superintendent, editor of the *Journal of Speculative Philosophy*, and soon-to-be U.S. Commissioner of Education. An intellectual who had confessed to his fiance, "I believe in no God as the popular mind does," Harris easily supported secular schools. He believed that morality had to be taught without religious indoctrination because Roman Catholics and modern science no longer permitted Protestant indoctrination. The day of unquestioning acceptance of religious authority had passed, Harris declared. Because educators now taught by demonstration and verification, religion—which urged faith instead of reason—had best be taught outside the schools. Reading the Bible as literature could continue in the *Appleton Reader*, Harris conceded, but not religious inculcation of faith.[7]

In teaching secular ethics, Harris insisted that teachers impose morality and this moral education began by requiring the mechanical virtues—punctuality, regularity, and silence. Children must be at school on time, respond to the bell, move in lines, have lessons finished on time, and restrain their animal impulses to prate and chatter. Repetition of these mechanical virtues indoctrinated children with self-control and self-sacrifice, making them receptive to their social duties, which Harris described as the cardinal virtues—temperance, prudence, fortitude, and justice—with the specific additions of industry, courtesy, truthtelling, and respect for law. Harris would indoctrinate children in all the secular virtues, but not in their religious duties—faith, hope, and charity—which should be left to the churches.[8]

Harris promoted moral education because he shared the fears of his college-educated generation that immigration, the Civil War, industrial change, and materialism undermined traditional moral authority. He was one of those mugwumps who had broken with Republicans in the 1884 revolt against the Grand Old Party's decline in moral virtue. Cynical modern historians have assumed that mugwump complaints were only the disappointments of an elite elbowed out of political power. Yet mugwumps were concerned with more than just office. Their three big issues—civil service reform, free trade, and sound money—were moral issues about which they had learned the truth in "moral philosophy," the college course the Age of Enlightenment had substituted for medieval theology. Moral philosophy assumed the existence of a general science of human nature which might be divided into the branches of ethics, psychology, aesthetics, politics, and political economy, but all of these were taught in a single senior-level course by the college president. Ever since Sir Isaac Newton published his *Mathematical Principles of Natural Philosophy* (1687) demonstrating that all motion of earth and the solar system could be described by the same mathematical formulas, educated men believed that human society must also be ruled by predictable natural laws. These laws had been laid out by eighteenth-century thinkers, especially Adam Smith and the Scottish common sense philosophy.[9]

Moral philosophy also taught that republics rested on civic virtue. A democracy which lacked a monarchy, aristocracy, or established church to compel obedience to the laws required its citizens to voluntarily place the common good ahead of selfish ends. The great purpose of moral philosophy was to inculcate moral character, the willingness to sacrifice individual interests to the greater good. In order to restrain the downward tendencies of appetite and passion which had ruined earlier civilizations, the truths of natural and revealed religion must be preserved. Even America was not free from the laws of history. Brown University President Francis Wayland warned that "it is vain for a people to expect to be free unless they are first willing to be virtuous."[10] To make this point, Wayland published *The Elements of Moral Science* (1835) and then *The Elements of Political Economy* (1837), offering the most popular packaging of classical theory as God's laws of economics.

But, some might ask, did not a greater diversity of political and economic ideas exist among moral philosophers? What about Francis Bowen and the tariff? It is true that Harvard College gave in to manufacturing interests in 1854 and hired an aggressive protectionist who dedicated his *Political Economy* (1856) to "Nathan Appleton, one of the most eminent living representatives of a highly honored class, the merchant princes of Boston. . . . " Bowen's heresy of government intervention to support New England manufacturing broke sharply with the consensus that had existed among moral philosophers, but this heresy persisted at Harvard for only one decade. President Charles W. Eliot brought his university back to the liberal consensus by hiring Charles F. Dunbar for a new chair of political economy in 1868. And the results of Civil War financing so shocked Francis Bowen that he moved back to orthodoxy.[11]

The Civil War had quickly given a refresher course to graduates in the truth of economic laws. The Legal Tender Act of 1862 was devastating for salaried professionals, who watched helplessly as the resulting greenback inflation cut their incomes in half. Congress had drafted this act in the second year of the Civil War: when it found the Federal treasury empty, it turned to paper money as the quickest way to refill it. Classical economic law taught that fiat paper money brought ruinous inflation, and though mugwump types cried out in protest, they were too patriotic to obstruct the financing of a war for freedom. By 1864, more than two greenbacks were required to purchase one gold dollar. Because the salaried man was paid with the depreciated notes and purchased all his commodities and services with them, his purchasing power was cut in half. As the cost of living rose, members of the community who lived on fixed incomes—salaries or annuities—found that they could afford only half the amount of food, clothing, housing, and education as had previously been within their means. They suffered months of personal austerity before prices hit their peak in 1868 and began to decline. During the fall of 1868, the *New York Times* said, "There never was a time in our history in which the salaried classes—accountants, clerks, teachers, professors and clergymen—were so poor."[12]

While inflationary paper money impoverished those on fixed incomes, it also seemed to ruin the moral character of businessmen. Merchants had once made their way to fortune by, according to E. L. Godkin, "patient, steady plodding, through early rising, plain living, and small economies", but the new age of inflation turned the business community toward speculation. The stock and gold markets provided the most flamboyant means of speculative wealth, but producers and holders of all goods found it easy to make profits during this period of rising prices. It was well known that money was made in the oil fields of Pennsylvania and Ohio, or by contracts for the Army, Navy, Indian Department, or even the lighthouse service. Men suddenly grew rich in a multitude of occupations. And in all businesses, rising prices gave the advantage to the more adventurous, the more speculative debtor-entrepreneur. When certain of these entrepreneurs corrupted legislatures and courts of law, mugwump moralists were outraged.[13]

Moral philosophers were specifically troubled by Jay Gould and Jim Fisk, who had been exposed by the journalism of young Henry Adams. Both were denounced by Adams as conspicuous examples of "a low and degraded moral and social type" who had risen suddenly on a flood of paper money to great power and wealth. Gould was born on a poor hill farm in Roxbury, New York, but by the outbreak of the Civil War this man with no conception of moral principle had moved from the tannery business to railroad speculation. His partner in vice, Jim Fisk, began as a peddler, rose to the jobbing business in Boston, and then moved into high finance at the close of the war. These speculators were no common sharpers. They joined forces with Daniel Drew, a director of the Erie Railroad, and managed such spectacular operations as looting stockholders and purchasing special legislation to legalize their fraud. They bought judges, political bosses, and the New York state legislature. The best of lawyers, David Dudley Field, a law reformer and the brother of a Supreme Court justice, willingly entered their pay. Even President Grant associated with Gould and Fisk, who exploited their contact to corner the gold market in the "black Friday" conspiracy. They bought a white marble palace in the style of European aristocrats and purchased Pike's Opera House on Eighth Avenue, which supplied Fisk with women enough for what Adams called a "permanent harem." With shameless ostentation Fisk rode around New York with his "batch of harlots." It seemed to Henry Adams that neither Honore Balzac nor Alexandre Dumas had ever depicted an instance of social mobility as striking as the rise of these two crooks. Adams could only hope that "Gould and Fisk will at last be obliged to yield to the force of moral and economical laws."[14]

After the financial panic of 1873, when Congress sneered at economic laws and voted to expand the money supply, a Yale professor of political economy, William Graham Sumner, rushed to press with a treatise on *The History of American Currency* (1874), which sought to restore respect for fundamental laws by looking back to British and American history. Sumner emphasized that paper money, from colonial days to the present, had always been disastrous, both morally and economically. Inflated currency caused a deterioration of public morals and a contempt for patient industry. Financially, it led to erratic heats and chills, and ended in ruin and repudiation. The British had spelled out the laws of money in the *Bullion Report* (1810), and nothing new had been discovered about the workings of paper money since. Like Newton's theory of the solar system, the doctrines had passed that state where the scientific financier was bound to debate them.[15]

Surely no other group remained so consistent on economic questions during the Gilded Age. Business shifted and divided over government intervention in the economy. Both political parties voted and maneuvered on the money question with their ears turned to voter demands rather than their eyes fixed on printed moral truth. Harvard's Charles Dunbar observed that Congress seemed to "drift upon a sea of doubt, without compass and without any directing impulse save such as may come from the veering gusts of popular feeling." Only on the tariff question did the parties show consistency, with the free-trade Democrats opposing Republican tariffs. For mugwump intellectuals in 1884, the Republican candidate James G. Blaine represented all the violations of moral philosophy—speculation, soft money, protective tariffs, and the political corruption of virtue. The Lincoln party, which had once stood for individual freedom, had ceased to represent moral virtue.[16]

To the common Anglo-American moral philosophy which all mugwumps shared, Harris added his own German idealism. Out in St. Louis, the New England transcendentalist had fallen in with a German Hegelian who reasoned that Hegel answered all Harris's problems with God and the state. How could pure individualism support the Federal Union's war on southern white individuals? How could philosophical belief in God be preserved? Hegel praised both the state and the individual and described human history as the evolving of God's reason. In the Hegelian view, education had the divine mission of shaping immoral little humans into ethical individuals in the movement from savagery to civilization. Capitalist society was no brutal struggle for self-interest but a division of labor based on love and justice. Each produced something useful not for himself but for others, and money payments merely measured an individual's contributions to society. Except for the artificially created Civil War millionaires, the rich did not grind the poor; rather, their innovations raised the standard of living for society. Harris marshaled statistics against those (Karl Marx, Henry George, and Edward Bellamy) who declared that the rich got richer while the poor increased in misery. The truth of statistics demonstrated that middle classes increased most rapidly as capitalist combinations reduced costs for consumers.[17]

The trouble with socialist versions of capitalism began with their slum perspective. They viewed the competitive system from amidst the weaklings of society—paupers, criminals, and those unable to compete—in the cities of New York and London. These socialists, according to principal Harris, rejected the traditional remedy of teaching the poor to become "industrious, economical, and skillful." The new socialist remedy proposed instead to abolish altogether the practice of thrift and character by prohibiting individual accumulation of property.

The Harris defense of possessive individualism reflected schoolteachers' applause of the capitalist system. Teachers, not preachers, were the group who gave uncompromising support to the status quo. Although the religious press regularly offered criticism of the economic system from a biblical perspective, the National Education Association offered sustained cheerleading. Teachers and administrators emotionally declared themselves against "socialism, communism, and the materialistic," while praising presidential power against protesting railroad strikers and populist farmers. Educator Harris believed his purpose was to prevent the minds of children and workers from being "flyblown with crazy political and social theories destructive of the state."[18]

Superintendent Harris, who believed that the drill of little habits laid the foundation of all moral character, used his first annual report as Commissioner of Education to reprint J. H. Thiry's "School Savings Banks in the United States." The school thrift movement really began with Thiry, an immigrant from Belgium who had left schoolteaching to make his fortune in business. Thiry had admired European school savings programs and, after his retirement on Long Island in the 1870s, he devoted himself to promoting thrift education in America. Beginning with a Long Island public school in 1885, Thiry persuaded the school board and principal to include a school bank as part of the educational program.[19]

In the Thiry school bank system the teacher took 15 minutes every Monday morning to call the class roll and ask each child to bring forward his or her weekly deposit. The coins carried to the teacher's desk were recorded in the roll book and on the individual student's savings card. At the end of roll call, all coins were counted, compared with the roll book total, sealed in an envelope, and carried to the principal. The principal then recorded class totals and sent the janitor to deposit the money in the school name with the local savings bank. Forms for all the necessary banking operations were offered by Thiry. Although there were other school savings systems (such as a stamp system in Baltimore borrowed from European benevolent societies), most school banks used the system promoted by Thiry.

When the Women's Christian Temperance Union (WCTU) endorsed school savings banks in 1890 and appointed Sara Louisa Oberholtzer to National Superintendent of School Savings Banks, the Thiry system received support from the largest women's organization of the nineteenth century. Mrs. Oberholtzer publicized the Thiry system as the best school bank system for preventing boys from becoming drunkards, wife beaters, and paupers. Where children were taught thrift, Mrs. Oberholtzer said, "extravagant, thoughtless habits, which begat inequality, drunkenness and vice, could not thrive. . . . If we could stimulate the poor to provident habits, and prove to the middle classes the foolishness of spending all as they get it, and to the greatest enjoyment, we would be exercising a broader and more healthful benevolence."[20]

School savings banks were clearly a benevolence movement to rescue the individual and society. John Thiry agreed with the WCTU that spending money in the hands of children had "brought many of our young people to the first step of the ladder of crime and pauperism. . . ."[21] If children were led away from spending for candy and pastries, by the "lessons of thrift and economy" they and society would enjoy the benefits of savings. Concern over the drunken abuse of women, the influx of immigrants, and the rise of labor radicalism all created support for school banking.

By 1890, school banking had spread to 31 eastern cities and 158 schools. Early school reports praised the effect on children. Mrs. Edith Cabot of the Boston suburb of Brookline, who supervised a school filled largely by Irish children of workingmen ("mainly day laborers"), reported that the students had given up candy and cakes. "Parents are much in the habit of paying their children for little services rendered," she wrote Commissioner Harris, "and this money is now brought to the penny savings instead of going to the candy shop." In the first three months, her 142 Brookline children had saved $42.54 and learned "forethought and self-control."[22]

Over the next 20 years—through the terrible depression of the 1890s and the inflationary good times of the progressive period—the number of school banks increased to 280. Still, that 280 represented a small minority of the nation's schools. To be sure, saving bank facilities were available only around the great cities, but rural and small town schools might have used the new Postal Savings Banks which opened in 1911 and permitted post offices to sell dime savings stamps to children and immigrants. Perhaps rural and small-town people had too little money to make regular banking practical. Teachers were also reluctant to take on the chores of a savings bank: Largely young and unmarried, teachers seem to have grown less attracted to thrift than to spending. They really didn't want to bother collecting pennies and nickels, so the leading advocates of school saving continued to come from outside the classroom. Savings bankers who had generally opposed the postal savings banks as unfair competition were very enthusiastic about the school banks in which they cooperated to develop a relationship with young savers. Bankers even secured state legislation promoting compulsory thrift education in the public schools in Massachusetts, New York, New Jersey, California, and Minnesota.[23]

The greatest advocate of school thrift was not a savings but a mortgage banker, Simon W. Straus, who created the American Society for Thrift in 1914. Straus did not need children's pennies. His innovation in mortgage banking had financed skyscrapers through real estate bonds, selling hundreds of millions through his S. W. Straus and Company. Straus's benevolent motivations were those of a dutiful son whose self-made father had, upon his death in 1898, left a letter urging Simon to carry on the work of thrift education. "I left home a poor boy of nineteen years," the Prussian-born father wrote, "worked very hard, and saved all the money I could, and in two and one-half years I saved up $500." The father had built the mortgage banking business in Chicago that Straus expanded to 50 cities. In 1914 in Chicago—carrying out his father's benevolent instruction to do good deeds—Simon organized the American Society for Thrift, which promoted school gardens and school banks. He secured the Education Bureau's blessings for a trip to Europe to gather information about thrifts, staged an International Congress for Thrift in San Francisco in 1915, and persuaded the National Education Association (NEA) to organize a committee on thrift and award prizes in his name to students who wrote the best thrift essays.[24]

The First World War in Europe, as well as Straus's vigor, made saving money a major topic at the 1916 NEA convention in New York City. The entire morning session preached thrift. Straus led the call to prepare for the difficult economic times which, he said, would follow the war even if we never entered the fighting. Americans were the most thriftless of all nations, he pointed out, with only 108 savings bank depositors for every 1,000 citizens (compared to Switzerland's 544). If we did not return to the colonial ways of Benjamin Franklin, then we might not survive as a nation. "We need but to read our histories," he declared. "Babylonia, Greece and Rome fell because their people were pampered, because debauchery ran riot, and their substance was wasted."[25]

Even as the NEA opened its convention to an emotional call for patriotic saving, the speakers' platform itself suggested that the bankers and middle-class reformers had not won their campaign to persuade teachers to become advocates of thrift. The only woman speaker, Kate Blake, a New York City principal, resented men preaching economy to women. She did not regard frugality as the desired goal of education, but spoke instead the new consumer language of "scientific management" for the home.[26] Spending rather than saving interested Ms. Blake and a growing number of consumers.

Apparently, including thrift sermons in education conventions and savings lessons in elementary curriculums illustrated not the triumph, but a last hurrah, of traditional economic wisdom. Public schools had been pressured into taking up an ethic that was already in trouble. Principal Blake's new language of scientific spending reflected emerging consumer assumptions in a maturing industrial nation. Advocacy of the new spending values would, of course, be delayed by war patriotism, but the unquestioned reign of thrift values had already ended.

6

Black Spenders

American slavery interrupted the African heritage of blacks, separating them from their traditional folk wisdom. Africans, like
all other agricultural peoples, had worked because survival and
tradition required it. Black children learned prudence proverbs:
"Poverty is the elder daughter of laziness," and "Dust on the
feet is better than dust on the behind."[1] Traditional cultural
beliefs in work and frugality made little sense in the American
system of slavery where individuals lacked control over their
and their families' futures. If no wealth could be accumulated
and passed on to children—if food, shelter, and retirement were
the responsibility of the master and not the slave—only immediate consumption and pleasure made any sense. The self-reliance of Afro-Americans was corroded under the paternalism of
slavery: the future belonged to the masters, and slaves had only
the present. Blacks preserved only those parts of African culture
that were still useful under slavery. The family, for example,
persisted because it could give love, affection, and self-esteem
in the present even though it was powerless to preserve anything
for the future.

The plantation South offered the poorest frugality instruction
in the western hemisphere. Rather than teaching a middle-class

ethic, the slave system promoted an aristocratic love of leisure, pleasure, and conspicuous consumption. Black Southerners learned to resent work. In the words of former slave Frederick Douglas it was the "close-fisted stinginess that fed the poor slave on coarse cornmeal and tainted meat" while the luxuries of the great house appeared like the pearly gates of heaven. Douglass believed planters were envied because of "their immense wealth, their gilded splendor, this profusion of luxury, this exemption from toil, this life of ease, this sea of plenty." The image of a big house being enjoyed by leisured, mint-julep-drinking ladies and gentlemen spoke volumes against steadiness, regularity, and sustained effort. Even slaveholders on small farms were viewed as consuming wealth, and the young Booker T. Washington grew up coveting ginger cake parties with young ladies.[2]

While plantation life culturally impoverished Afro-Americans, the cracker culture of poor whites offered no model of the thrifty yeoman. If Celtic interpretations of Old South culture are true, "Celt and Southerners were simply too lazy, too unstable, too migratory and too committed to sensual pleasures to be yeomen. Indeed, the desire to enjoy a leisurely life and all the pleasures possible, without laboring, were characteristic of both Celts and Southerners and set them apart from most Englishmen and Yankees." Whiskey, hunting, fishing, fighting, gambling, and the pleasures of table and bed all ranked higher with Southerners— white and black—than money, education, or ambition. "Now, I never calculate to save anything," a typical Southerner declared in *Cracker Culture*, "I tell my wife . . . I mean to enjoy what I earn as fast as it comes." Habits of frugality, discipline, work, and piety may well have been such uncommon traits among Southerners that most could have been fairly described as "neither thrifty nor prudent."[3]

Among the ten percent of Afro-Americans who were free before the Civil War, a more frugal capital accumulation was not uncommon. Free blacks had more disciplined, Scotch-Irish-Presbyterian role models in the southern towns. Well-to-do blacks accumulated property not only in Baltimore, but also in Natchez, Mississippi, where William Johnson accumulated a fortune of $20 to 30 thousand from barbering and real estate investments.

Prosperous blacks existed among the free population, living the Protestant ethic and recommending during the Civil War that freed slaves "shape their course toward frugality, the accumulation of property, and above all, to leave untried no amount of effort and self-denial to acquire knowledge, and to secure a vigorous moral and religious growth."[4]

The liberating Union army brought along a crusade of Northern, white schoolteachers to preach Yankee civilization in black freedmen's school. The missionaries came intending to produce ebony puritans who would cultivate self-discipline, save money, and buy land. *The Freedman*, a new textbook series written specifically to include blacks as middle-class role models, may have been used less frequently than the old McGuffey Readers and Webster's Spellers, which were donated by book publishers. But from all these texts, southern freedmen received the same moral instruction that had dominated northern education before the Civil War.[5]

The savings bank came south in the same Yankee carpetbags as the McGuffey Readers. John W. Alvord, a Connecticut-born Congregational minister, abolitionist, and teacher who had joined the Freedmen's Bureau to educate former slaves called together New York philanthropists in the last year of the war to organize a savings bank for blacks. This bank was supposed to teach blacks the same self-discipline, thrift, independence, pride, and self-respect that northern workingmen were believed to have learned from their banks. The thrift reformers petitioned Congress to approve their charter for a mutual savings bank and then launched a crusade against poverty and dependence among the freedmen.[6]

Alvord personally promoted the Freedman's Savings and Trust Company. Organizing branches in 15 central places the first year, he told cashiers that "the real improvement of these people . . . depends on their individual thrift. . . . Be cashier and preacher." As Inspector of Schools and Finances for the Freedmen's Bureau, as well as secretary of the Freedman's Bank, Alvord appeared as an official government spokesman for frugality and savings. In the South, he found a sympathetic audience among urban blacks who had been free before the war, including "mechanics, keepers of groceries and wood-yards, butchers, market men and women, owing their own dwellings, in the town or its suburbs, and some with small plantations." Even lower-class blacks, he reported, often saved coins in secret boxes and were eager to hear how bank interest could help purchase a homestead. Alvord assured the government that, with the industry of blacks now assisted by the savings bank, "Pauperism can be brought to a close, the freedmen made self-supporting and prosperous, paying for their educational and Christian institutions, and helping to bear the burdens of government by inducing habits of saving in what they earn. That which savings banks have done for the working men of the north it is presumed they are capable of doing for these laborers."[7]

To promote deposits, Alvord's bank recruited support from Freedmen's Bureau teachers, black ministers, and political leaders. The bank also published instructional advertising tracts. One such booklet, *Reasons Why You Should All Put Money in the Savings Bank* listed the six reasons for deposits:

1. *Because it is your surest way to get a start in life.* Thousands of rich men would have been poor all their lifetime had they not used the Savings Bank.

2. *Because, being your own masters, it is your duty to provide for your settlement in life, for your families, for sickness, and for old age.* You can in no way do this so well as by a monthly deposit in a good Savings Bank.

3. *It teaches you the value of money,* and prevents you from spending it foolishly.

4. *You should use this Bank* because it is conducted entirely by your best friends, and it is hoped you will, ere long, help to conduct it yourselves; and being authorized by Congress, and approved by the President of the United States, it is the safest place you can find for your money.

5. *It gives you character.* As soon as you become worth a little money or property, every one begins to respect you and ask your advice.

6. *It is a good example of thrift to your children,* whom you desire to see respected and prosperous citizens. They will be sure to imitate your example.[8]

Bank propaganda targeted the consumption ethic for special criticism. Giving in to the appetites—rich food, flashy clothing, tobacco, whiskey, and gambling—led to disaster and pauperism. Self-restraint, on the other hand, won pride, respect, and financial security. Bank morality propaganda advised:

If you work hard you will earn money the same as other folks. Not one of you need remain poor if you are careful and do not spend money for candy, or whiskey, or costly clothes. As for food, cheap, hearty victuals—beef, fish, bread, coffee—will do for men and women better than pies, cakes, and such things which cost more money and give you less strength.

Tobacco and *whiskey* are the two things which all men who are going to save money must neither touch nor taste.

Let us count the cost of a cigar and a glass of whiskey every working day. A mean cigar costs five cents, and the poorest glass of whiskey five cents, which makes ten cents. Now if instead of worse than wasting this, you would save it every day—one Dime per day—at the end of one year . . . amounts to thirty-one dollars and twenty cents. . . . Put it in the bank at six per cent interest and it will grow, with continued savings, to $411.13 in ten years.

And all this from saving the price of a mean cigar and a vile glass of liquor every day! There is no excuse for any healthy man being poor in this country.

But the worst of it is yet to tell: if you had spent the ten cents a day in tobacco and whiskey, you would not only not have had the $411.13 at the ten years end, but also had bad habits. Very likely you would have become a drunkard, and spent not five but fifty cents a day, if you could get them, for the drunkard's cup. Your family would be ragged; your wife miserable, and perhaps heartbroken; your children growing up in vices, with no chance to learn to read or write.

But, on the other hand, the very fact of saving the money will bring with it the pleasure, pride in yourself, good habits, good health, a good name, steady employment. All people will trust you. Man will point you out and say—"There's a sober, hard-working, honest man, with money ahead; you can trust him." So, too, will your wife be proud of you, and your children will respect you and grow up willing and obedient. They will all join to aid you in saving.[9]

For eight years, the Freedman's Bank preached frugality to the delight of black activists and capitalists such as Frederick Douglass, who thrilled as the bank worked "to instill into the minds of the untutored Africans lessons of sobriety, wisdom, and economy, and to show them how to rise in the world. Like snowflakes in winter, circulares, tracts and other papers were, by this benevolent institution, scattered among the sable millions . . . and as a result, money to the amount of millions flowed into its vaults." Douglass entrusted his $12 thousand to the bank, thinking that the accumulated wealth of blacks would bring more consideration and respect for the race. He took pride in peeking through the window of the Washington, D.C. bank as he "looked down the row of its gentlemanly and elegantly dressed colored clerks, with their pens behind their ears and buttonhole bouquets in their coat-fronts, and left my very eyes enriched."[10]

Unfortunately, while the bank was preaching thrift to blacks, its home office had moved out from under the watchful eye of frugal New Yorkers to Washington, D.C. and the extravagant control of speculative banker Henry D. Cooke. Cooke turned freedmen's savings into risky real estate mortgages, as well as bonds and notes of his brother's Jay Cooke and Company. His extravagant management included constructing an elegant new bank building that cost more than a quarter million dollars. Inevitably, the bank became insolvent after the 1873 financial panic, and fewer than half the 61,000 depositors were able to turn in their bank books and obtain 62 cents on the dollar for their deposits.[11]

Yankee advocates of thrift were shocked by the bank collapse which threatened to reverse the lessons of industry, thrift, and the morality of self-restraint. Failure of the Freedman's Bank was especially distressing because the honor of the federal government seemed to be involved. Congress had permitted the shameful practice of lending money for worthless securities. Only by reimbursing a million dollars of depositor losses could national honor and black faith in thrift be restored. The historian of American savings banks, Emerson Keyes, declared that the "shameful" congressional regulation should be wiped out by federal reimbursement of depositors. Reimbursement won the approval of a House Committee on Banking and the Controller of the Currency, but no relief was ever given, even though depositors continued to petition for 50 years.[12]

Reconstruction had ended by 1876 and the federal government abandoned special support for blacks. Congress refused to do

any more for a black bank than a failed white one. White abo-
litionists generally supported federal reimbursement, but even
among them the tide had generally turned against further government intervention in the South. The Civil War amendments
and civil rights laws had established equality; now blacks must
look to themselves rather than to government. The question of
demonstrating racial equality, John G. Whittier said, rested on
"whether by patient industry, sobriety, and assiduous self-cul-
ture, they shall over come the unchristian prejudice still existing
against them, or by indolence, thriftlessness, and moral and
physical degradation they shall confirm and strengthen it."[13]

The lessons of frugality and thrift had been damaged, but not
undone, by the Freedman's Bank—which had handled some $57
million and lost but a single million. Some theorize that the evil
influence of failure undermined thrift for generations, but there
was evidence of large black deposits in white southern banks
within two years of the Freedman's collapse. Unquestionably,
the collapse had no direct impact on most blacks: Most had never
been depositors because they lived outside the few urban centers
where the Freedman's Bank and Yankee schoolteachers taught
thrift. Some 100,000 blacks had once deposited money in the
bank, and 60,000 lost money at the end, but what of the 4 million
who had made no use of the Bank?

The typical Afro-American lived in the rural South under the
paternalism of sharecropping. Freedom had given blacks more
personal space as they moved their cabin from the old slave
quarters to an individual plot of land. They no longer lived
directly under the eye of the white planter or labored in the gang
labor system of slavery, but under freedom, the land—and usually the mule, plow, and seed—still belonged to the planter. The
sharecropper claimed only half his crop and had as little control
over his agriculture as his money. He lived on credit from the
furnishing merchant at the plantation store, buying only in that
one store and taking only what the merchant agreed to let him
have at credit prices inflated from 24 percent to grand theft.
Moving from slavery to sharecropping, blacks generally increased their share of agricultural income from 22 to 56 percent,
and now bought luxury goods such as canned peaches and Sunday suits, but they had not gained the self-reliance of free people.

Sharecroppers were kept in hopeless debt bondage to the furnishing merchants and landlords who controlled their lives and spending. The credit system perpetuated improvident and careless habits. W. E. B. Du Bois observed; "They are careless because they have not found it pays to be careful; they are improvident because the improvident ones of their acquaintance get on about as well as the provident." In the Georgia black belt, Du Bois found 89 percent of blacks living without hope of emerging from debt. Only 5 percent had risen to money renters and 6 percent to landowners by the end of the century.[14]

Paternalism and its shiftless peasantry were the social evils that black education sought to overthrow. Northern missionaries had followed the Union armies to teach the Yankee doctrines of individual self-reliance. Yankee General Samuel C. Armstrong stayed on in Virginia to establish the best-known industrial school, Hampton Institute. The son of Presbyterian missionaries, Armstrong had grown up in Hawaii, where he learned that the education of Polynesians (and other backward races) should consist of moral and manual training rather than intellectual instruction. Backward races must first assimilate the values and skills of Yankee civilization. If they mastered trades, worked hard, bought land, saved money, and created stable Christian families, they could evolve toward equality. At Hampton, the General told his students: "Be thrifty and industrious. Command the respect of your neighbors by a good record and a good character. Own your own houses. Educate your children. Make the best of your difficulties."[15]

Hampton's most famous pupil, Booker T. Washington, learned the Yankee lessons well during his three years with Armstrong and the New England lady teachers. Washington went on to build his own Tuskegee Institute in Alabama and, declaiming that thrift and toil and savings were the highway to progress and equality, he gained a reputation as black America's leading orator. Washington climaxed the Yankee missionary gospel of thrift and piety to black America. Individuals and civilizations who succeeded were those who saved time and money, Booker emphasized in his Sunday evening Tuskegee chapel talks: "We cannot get upon our feet, as a people, until we learn the saving habit; until we learn to save every nickel, every dime and every dollar that we can spare." Saving money required self-control, the ability to say no: "I want you to be able to go by a store and, as you notice the things in that store—whether candy or spring hats, or whatever it is that attracts you—to be able, notwithstanding the fact that you have the money in your pockets to buy, to exercise a self-control that will enable you to pass these things by and save your money to invest it in a house." Saving should not be postponed until after marriage; all young people should save: "Resolve that no matter how little you may earn, you will put a part of the money in the bank. If you earn four dollars a week, put two dollars in the bank. If you earn ten dollars, save four of them. Put the money in the bank. Let it stay there. When it begins to drawn interest you will find that you will appreciate the value of money."[16]

Booker's message of economic self-sufficiency was shared by virtually all black leaders at the turn of the century. Professor W. E. B. Du Bois spoke for black capitalism and savings bank frugality. Religious leaders, such as Reverend E. C. Morris, president of the National Baptist Convention, advised:

Let every man among us get a home, improve it, and then add to that a good bank account. Go into the unbroken forest, buy forty, sixty or a hundred acres of land, build a house, move into it and stay there until the last dollar of the purchase price has been paid. Never come to town, except on business, and then to sell rather than to buy. Let the politician, the office-seeker and the merchant look for you, instead of you looking for them.[17]

In Arkansas, black farmers had taken advantage of undeveloped land, and 23 percent were landowners. By 1910 almost 40 percent of tenants owned farming equipment and paid cash rather than shares of their crops for rent. Across the South, evidence of property accumulation illustrates that blacks were accumulating property more rapidly that southern whites. In Georgia, freedmen who had started out in 1865 with nothing had by 1880 acquired $8 per capita, a figure representing one thirty-sixth of the local white per capita wealth. By 1910, the average Georgia black had $26.59. Although the dollar amount might seem insignificant, Robert Higgs has described the relative

gain on whites as "tremendous." In just 30 years, black ownership of real estate, livestock, and household furnishings had
risen from one thirty-sixth to one-sixteenth that of whites. Property assessments in five southern states demonstrated that the
assessed value of black wealth accumulated more rapidly than
that of whites. Southern blacks apparently practiced frugality
and thrift more than southern whites during the years 1865 to
1915.[18]

The age of Booker T. Washington might appear to be a new
era of thrift and landownership, but in fact the age marked an
end to black accumulation. As the course of agriculture ran
against the small family farm, the percentage of landless tenants
grew. Especially significant for blacks, however, was the great
migration north that began when job opportunities opened during the First World War. Thrifty blacks especially sold out to
whites and moved to northern cities for greater freedom, economic opportunity, and higher education for their children.
After 1916, black wealth in the South plummeted as landowners
sold their property to whites and joined the great migration to
northern cities.

Blacks entered urban America with less resistance to the consumer culture than any other ethnic group. Although frugal,
landowning black families had indoctrinated their children with
Booker's methodical habit of saving forty (or at least ten) percent
of their incomes, the great landless majority had not. Sharecroppers surely had no occasion to instruct their children to
"make a dollar, save a dime," thereby urging a regular saving
of ten percent. Sharecroppers who had lived all their lives on
credit moved to Chicago with higher hopes for city credit than
for the Urban League's Thrift Week sermons on the value of
savings and budget making.

Even among the migrating middle class, E. Franklin Frazier
has argued, the stronger puritanical tradition proved insufficient
to protect against mindless consumerism. Feelings of inferiority
created by life in a prejudiced white nation were apt to seek
compensation by purchases of Cadillacs, jewelry, flashy clothing, and recognition on the society page. Frazier's sour commentary might seem to be a variety of the traditional puritanism
that literary intellectuals ridiculed in the twenties while they

admired Harlem and the black lifestyle precisely because they did not represent temperance, industry, frugality, and chastity. But Frazier was no traditional moralist seeking to accumulate capital in the middle class. He was an economic radical angry because the black bourgeoisie had failed to provide radical leadership for the black masses.[19]

American cultural values gradually shifted against criticism of black spending. The old racist style of British individualism had lamented that "the negro has yet to learn the first elements of Anglo-Saxon thrift." But as Nazi racism in Germany tarnished the use of race and Keynesian economics repudiated thrift and self-reliance, the modern liberalism of Gunnar Myrdal's *An American Dilemma* rejected all moral criticism. We are all guilty of conspicuous consumption, this Carnegie Foundation study said, and our response to black prodigality should be "more education, better housing, increased economic security—not moral indignation." Myrdal's sociology even used a faulty study that proved blacks more careful budgeters than whites. Racist notions about black improvidence were therefore declared "greatly exaggerated," but the liberal study assigned no real importance to the habit of savings.[20]

Since the 1930s, black thrift propaganda has found its greatest advocates among those who reject American culture. Consider the message of Elijah Muhammed, who preached that "debt is slavery." He urged his people:

Stop spending money for tobacco, dope, cigarettes, whiskey, fine clothes, fine automobiles, expensive rugs and carpets, idleness, sport and gambling. Stop ... living on credit loans ... seeking the highest price merchandise. ... If you must have a car, buy the low-priced car. ... We must make a better future for ourselves and our children.[21]

The rigorous self-discipline of the Muslims was a rebellion against American and black consumption, but few blacks ever became Muslims. Selling self-restraint in post–World War II America ran counter to a culture of self-indulgence. When West Indian immigrants demonstrated an industriousness and frugality in American ghettos, they won the slightly derisive label, "black Jews." To be sure, notable examples of black thrift existed in every community, but the cultural norm of the television generation was immediate consumption. In the 1980s almost one-third of all black families had no net worth, and in every income group, blacks saved far less than other Americans. In a nation of consumers, blacks were the best spenders.[22]

7

The War Savings Movement

Democratic governments claim that values come from the people. American theory teaches that voters elect representatives to reflect the virtues of the public, to voice the moral wisdom of the majority. Popular politicians are therefore reluctant to criticize an electorate for lack of character. Only once did American government launch a major educational campaign against the profligate, spendthrift habits of Americans. That campaign grew out of a fear for national safety when the United States entered World War I. The architects of the National War Savings Movement intended something more than a temporary defense program, however. They sought a permanent reformation of American character.

For a decade before the European war, editorial writers worried over rising prices and the thriftless spending of Americans. Older traditionalists worried that advertising had turned America from a nation of thrifty people into one of reckless consumers whose pursuit of goods, display, and spending had driven prices one-third higher during a single decade. But neither editorials nor the American Society for Thrift had any effect on the inflationary price spiral that doubled the cost of food staples. In February 1917, angry housewives rioted in New York City, overturning food carts and marching on City Hall, demanding cheap food. Prices became a concern of government. After America declared war on April 16, President Woodrow Wilson entered the campaign against inflation by attacking excessive consumption and urging thrift; "This is the time for America to correct her unpardonable fault of wastefulness and extravagance. Let every man and woman assume the duty of careful, provident use and expenditure as a public duty, as a dictate of patriotism."[1]

The thrift movement gained support from testimony by Britain about its economy campaign. Britain had been fighting a terrible total war for three years when the United States joined the struggle. British treasury official Basil P. Blackett came to America in the summer of 1917 and explained that the need for goods and services for the war had compelled his government to push consumers out of the market by persuading them against buying. To reverse English consumers' traditional disdain for the mean habit of saving (proper only to parsimonious Scotland), the British National War Savings Committee portrayed wartime extravagance and waste as "treason"—spilling the blood of heroes when goods and services were diverted from the battlefront. London posters proclaimed: "To dress extravagantly in wartime is not only unpatriotic—it is bad form." And: "Don't ride in a motor car for pleasure." Across Britain, citizens enlisted in local committees to sell thrift and British savings certificates.[2]

At a July 19, 1917 conference with Federal Reserve banking officials, Blackett explained that American efforts to finance the war through Liberty Bonds could never soak up the buying power of most consumers because the minimum $50 Liberty Bond was too expensive for most Americans. For laborers, women, and children, a $5 certificate must be offered, along with a government program of propaganda to take consumers out of the competition for goods and services.[3]

A nine-page report from the banking officials moved Treasury Secretary William Gibbs McAdoo to appoint a committee on August 1 to work on a war savings campaign. Within a week, the Treasury Department had studied examples of savings stamp books used by schoolchildren and drafted proposed legislation authorizing $2 billion of small savings certificates. By September 25, Congress had approved the sale of savings certificates, and

McAdoo appointed Frank Vanderlip to head the department's new National War Savings Division.

Like a character out of a Horatio Alger novel, Vanderlip began life as an Illinois small-town and farm boy, entered Chicago journalism, moved on to the Treasury Department during the Spanish American War, and then to Wall Street banking. He consistently saved money from his salary until an investment in Texas land made him a millionaire at age 45. As the outspoken president of New York City's National City Bank, he appeared on a Liberty Loan speakers' platform with Herbert Hoover and the entire Wilson cabinet, and he drew more applause and newspaper coverage than anyone else. "We are a nation of spenders and we must learn to economize," Vanderlip declared. "It is unpatriotic to spend money for anything but necessities now. . . . Men engaged in producing luxuries should cease at once as a patriotic act." The Wilson administration needed support from hostile Wall Street, so Vanderlip was offered the new Savings Division of Treasury. As a patriotic American who believed in thrift, he was eager to abandon his $100,000-a-year bank salary to become a dollar-a-year man in the war government.[4]

On September 25, Vanderlip began work in a small, dingy, inside room on the second floor of the Treasury building. A member of the power structure, he easily organized a Washington conference of top executives from banking, insurance, manufacturing, distribution, and labor for October 12, where he explained the details of his Savings Division plans and asked for criticism and support. Vanderlip candidly told representatives from Sears and Montgomery Ward, who were interested in the approaching Christmas buying season: "We want to spoil as much Christmas trade as possible. Those of you who are in merchandising are shocked, no doubt. That is the lesson of thrift we have to learn."[5] With only a hint of complaint, the conference participants offered support for the patriotic effort to reduce consumption.

With the approval of major economic interests, Vanderlip could build an organization to reach every local community in America. State volunteer directors, usually bankers, were called to Washington for a November 15–16 pep talk from Vanderlip, Secretary McAdoo, and President Wilson—who asked them to

help win the war and also promote one of the greatest byproducts of the war, the lesson of thrift. "There is no more important
movement in America today than this movement for savings
and economy," McAdoo declared. A simple, little thrift card was
going to raise $2 billion, Vanderlip said, and even better, it was
"going to teach thrift to America." Vanderlip continued: "We
have not stood up very well under that hardest test of all—
prosperity. We have become careless, we have become a
spendthrift people. Our savings do not compare per capita with
those of poorer countries. Sweden has five times as much saving
per capita as we have in this country. So has Switzerland."[6]

By creating state organizations to persuade citizens to abandon
nonessential consumption and use the money instead to buy
savings stamps, the directors could build character, encourage
virtue, and strengthen the nation. They could use the incentive
of patriotism to persuade others to join the state organizations—
recruiting organizers in every county, every city, every school.
The War Saving Societies would promote saving and the patriotic
willingness to forego immediate gratifications in order to help
America.

Directors returned home from the conference to organize their
own states and deliver their own patriotic oratory. Dwight W.
Morrow, for example, the J. P. Morgan and Company executive
appointed New Jersey State War Savings Chairman, took for his
patriotic text President Wilson's statement, "It is not an army
that we must shape and train for war; it is a nation." Wars were
no longer battles won simply with physical force. Modern war
required "battles of whole nations. They are battles in which
organization plays a most important part. They are battles in
which thrift or lack of thrift may be the determining factor in
the final result." Wars were fought with goods and services,
and war saving was a movement to release goods to the government by reducing consumption. The Treasury asked people
to save their pennies, nickels, dimes, and quarters and regularly
buy thrift stamps. But the war savings movement was not pri-
marily a drive for money. It was asking people to reduce their
consumption and buy stamps with the savings. "In this country
millions and millions are yearning for an opportunity to do something in this war," Morrow said, "to deny themselves, to sac-

rifice, to do without what others may have. The War Savings movement is an answer to that yearning. It brings to every man, woman and child the opportunity to help."[7]

Vanderlip did not turn the campaign entirely over to his state organizations, however. He built a large Washington staff to promote the thrift gospel through media publicity and national organizations. While Vanderlip asked illustrators and editors to help get the thrift message across, his publicity section created and distributed thrift propaganda to the nation's newspapers and magazines. Ten people in the national organizations section communicated directly with women's clubs, labor unions, corporations, chambers of commerce, religious denominations, Boy Scouts, Rotarians, YMCAs, and every other group, including the schools.[8] Between Vanderlip's overlapping national and state War Savings organizations, few citizens failed to hear the message before the savings stamps went on sale in post offices and banks on December 3.

The thrift and frugality message immediately drew opposition from retail merchants across America, merchants who had earlier been miffed by Mrs. Wilson and the cabinet wives' "simple life" movement, which asked women to "pledge themselves to buy inexpensive clothing and simple food and to watch and prevent all kinds of waste." In nearly every city, opposition placards warning against too much economy appeared in retail store windows: "Business as Usual. Beware of Thrift and Unwise Economy." Merchants did not want their Christmas trade spoiled and gave Vanderlip's December campaign "twenty million damnings." Newspapers commonly reflected the opposition of their merchant advertisers, and "Business as Usual" editorials applauding normal buying ran from Boise to Boston. Hostile Boston press editorials and advertisements against thrift that continued into the spring of 1918 so offended a group of Cambridge professors that they wrote a patriotic letter of protest. When the Boston papers refused to print their protest, they hired an attorney who sought to purchase advertising space for the thrift policy recommended by Wilson, McAdoo, and Vanderlip. Only one of three Boston papers, the *Evening Transcript*, would sell space for four patriotic advertisements.[9]

Newspapers and retail merchants were not alone in opposing

thrift. Manufacturers who produced luxury automobiles did not want thrift to hurt their sales and hired advertisers to portray their grand machines as the very soul of thrift and frugality. Even bankers were not enthusiastic: Reports persistently found bankers fearful that savings stamps hurt bank deposits and that too much free work was expected of bankers in offering savings certificates for sale. With a few notable exceptions, bankers were reported to be "very unsympathetic" to the war savings campaign.[10]

To overcome the opposition, Vanderlip's campaign built a patriotic mass movement. War Savings may not have had posters as dramatic as those of the Liberty Loan and the Red Cross, and the Division was limited to selling only one thousand dollars of certificates to any individual, but it could become the patriotic movement of the people—the women, children, and working class.

The schools were exploited as the quickest way to the mass of Americans. "We are going to start this campaign through the schools," Vanderlip told Connecticut leaders, "because our two hundred and fifty thousand school children in the state can carry that idea home directly to the parents." To reach the children, he appealed to the teachers with flattery: "The school teacher is the pioneer outpost of the Government, standing at the threshold of the nation's homes. The schools of America are the single units where a national resolution can form and spread overnight into every household." Teachers responded to Vanderlip's patriotic appeal by rallying children around the flag and the savings stamp. "We must save money that we may save lives," children were told as they were handed individual Thrift Cards on which their names were written and to which they were to paste 25-cent stamps in the 16 numbered squares. The card itself might be considered a piece of advertising copy, for each square contained a pithy aphorism from Benjamin Franklin on the wisdom of saving. Once a week, teachers were asked to turn their schoolrooms into Savings Stamp markets, collecting nickels, dimes, and quarters in exchange for Savings Stamps. Children responded by sending millions of dollars to Washington. In the first month, the New York City schools sold $41 thousand dollars' worth of stamps.[11]

Some of the school programs were no doubt gentle with children, leading them in singing cute little ditties such as: *Little Ja-pa-nee Save-a-his money. Never waste a cent like A-mer-i-can; He can live so cheap But he save a heap. Ne-ver-be-broke like A-mer-i-can.* Charming little plays were performed, such as "Good Fairy Thrift" in which the wicked witch Wastefulness ruined American home and country until the good fairy Thrift appeared to save the land. Then the children sang:

SAVE UP YOUR PENNIES

1. There's a good old saying
That everybody knows
You hear it all around the globe
And this is how it goes
chorus
Save up your pennies for a rainy day
It's not always what you earn but what you put away.
Uncle Sam has need of thrift
So do your best, and give him a lift
and save your pennies for a rainy day.

2. Among the world's best nations
If we're to take a place
We must all learn a lesson of thrift
or never win the race.[12]

School pressure could quickly turn vicious toward those who failed to buy. In Minneapolis, Harrison Salisbury recalled, when Marie brought no money on stamp day—and even flippantly asserted that her mother had no money for savings—Harrison reported the delinquent to his father. That night the elder Salisbury dressed in his Home Guard uniform and organized a delegation to call on the girl's mother, who ran a rooming house. The next Friday, Marie bought four stamps for her card. Failure to buy stamps led patriots to assume you were pro-German: if you refused, you were a "pro" and were forced to purchase stamps to prove your patriotism.[13]

Selling pressures from school competed with that of the Boy Scouts and the War Savings Society in the workplace, church, fraternal order, and neighborhood. The Scouts were assigned five million pledge cards for soliciting signed stamp orders. A

Scout turning $25 worth of orders over to his local post office received an Achievement Button. For selling $250 worth of orders, he was promised a WSS Ace Medal. The 320,000 Scouts were told to think of themselves as modern Paul Reveres coming to the aid of their country. Scout propaganda boasted: "The Scouts are after the Kaiser's scalp, 320,000 strong."[14]

Across America, 140,000 War Savings Societies organized to pressure individuals into taking the thrift pledge and making regular purchases of stamps. A large metropolitan area, such as Atlantic City, might have 103 separate societies. The small town of Ridgefield Park, with not quite 2,000 citizens, needed only one organization of 110 women who divided and sold with military precision. The chairperson took $4 to 5 thousand dollars of stamps on credit from the bank every Tuesday and divided them among her nine captains, each of whom administered an assigned section of town with the assistance of lieutenants who called on every home and reported back at noon Friday.[15]

In towns and urban areas, individuals were brought under the eye of self-appointed censors of extravagance. Congress had prohibited distilling liquor, the Hoover Food Commission forbade fine eating, and Sunday automobile driving was under attack by War Saving patriots who promoted "gasless Sundays." In rural America, the societies were less applicable to a dispersed population without a weekly income, but patriots in Nebraska invented a coercive plan so effective that the National War Savings organization recommended it to other states. All taxpayers were called to the local schoolhouse and asked to buy stamps. Naturally, patriots shifted from persuasion to coercion in the case of "tightwads" and "slackers" who failed to show up. Complaints of coercion flooded into the national office from farmers who had been assessed $50 stamp pledges and told they must pay or appear before a local "council of defense." Of course, the Treasury told overzealous salesmen that "the purchase of War Savings Stamps is not compulsory."[16]

The worst coercion cases seemed to come as a result of the National War Savings Day drive which President Wilson proclaimed for June 28, 1918. After the President urged that "the people as evidence of their loyalty, invest all they can save in

Liberty Bonds and War Savings Stamps," patriots ignored traditions of individual freedom, not only in the American West,
but in New York City. When an uncooperative young man, Louis
Sotsky, declined to sell stamps, he was threatened that his draft
status would be changed. By the summer of 1918, the War Savings movement was less an educational effort than a patriotic
crusade which had silenced critics of thrift. The patriotic intolerance came not from the Washington War Savings Division but
from local organizations. Locals actually complained of the tepid
WSS posters and called for more bloody propaganda depicting
German frightfulness. "The principle of art may well be sacrificed somewhat," Ohio leaders said, "for stern facts, based on
the realization that the way to win this war is to get down in
the mud and *lick the Hun*."[17]

War Savings moved in triumph during the summer of 1918.
Stamp sales reached $211 million a month and Vanderlip could
declare that "opposition [had] pretty substantially disappeared."
Savings stamps were sold not only in the 55,000 post offices but
in 217,000 other licensed factories, businesses, banks, and financial institutions. The newspapers and magazines all carried
thrift propaganda, the schools were frugality factories, and war
saving had become the fashion even more than victory gardening. According to Frank Vanderlip, he and the War Savings
Division had "put thrift in uniform," making it a patriotic obligation to which an estimated 34 million citizens responded—
one-third of the population and easily the great majority of
American families. But Director Vanderlip came to regret that
the program had been diverted from education into just another
selling campaign. Liberty Loans, the intended money collector,
had raised $17 billion from banks and the rich, while War Savings
stamps contributed only $1 billion. But the purpose of the
broadly democratic stamp movement had been to soak up consumption funds and teach thrift. When stamp sales fell drasti-
cally after the cease-fire in the fall of 1918, habits of Americans
seemed not really changed by stamp-selling drives, and Vanderlip hoped that the Treasury program might become a permanent thrift education project. With double-digit inflation
roaring because the Wilson government chose an expanded
money supply over taxation, heavy consumer spending still

seemed unwise even after the war ended. When Vanderlip and Secretary McAdoo resigned and returned to civilian life in the fall of 1918, they urged a continuation of the Savings Division.[18]

The newly appointed Treasury Secretary, Carter Glass, worried even more than McAdoo had about thriftless Americans. Savings had fallen sharply once the guns in Europe were silenced by the armistice, and the delirium of war patriotism that had supported Treasury appeals for money quickly faded. Secretary Glass insisted, "The war is not over, as everyone seems to think." Two million American soldiers were still in Europe and the U.S. government continued to spend $2 billion a month. Thrift education had to continue, Glass insisted, "to impress upon the American people the necessity of cultivating the habits of thrift and savings. . . . Americans do not know what thrift is— what savings is. . . . The average European nation could live on what we waste."[19] Glass extended generous financing of the Savings Division and personally wrote letters to Christian ministers and schoolchildren.

The Savings Division was not without allies in its campaign for thrift education. The Young Men's Christian Association (YMCA) had its own program, and the savings banks that had pushed thrift for years were eager to take over all school banking programs. Young Savings Division executives were inclined to be a little cynical about the effectiveness of the banks, however. After a hundred years of selling thrift, the savings institutions had failed to make the virtue popular. These bankers were considered self-interested old conservatives, too traditional for modern promotions and too jealous of Treasury to be of much assistance.[20]

The YMCA ran a program in cooperation with the bankers. The Y, which had added thrift to its religious concerns during the war, continued to support the cause through a National Thrift Week in January, declaring thrift a fundamental part of character development: "The Association has come to see that habits of wastefulness and extravagance rot character. They make a man poor, they rob him of his judgment, steal his health and undermine his integrity. Most of the evils that beset and ruin the individual go back to the gaining, dividing and use of money." To promote their "Christian Financial Creed" of work,

budget, homeownership, bank, insurance, securities, and shar-
ing, the YMCA held meetings, distributed literature, and asked
ministers to preach on thrift, offering them a choice of three
printed sermon outlines. The first was a straight explanation of
the Y's Christian Financial Creed. The second was an evangelical, "owe no man anything but to love one another" denun-
ciation of debt: "Thriftlessness—debt—mars and stains the soul
so that it loses its value to us . . . to our fellowmen and god."
And the third was a postmillennial sermon that Jesus had come
to establish an ethical kingdom on earth, to eliminate the selfishness of extravagance.[21] The sermons and YMCA posters
quoting John Wesley ("Make all you can. Save all you can. Give
all you can") continued traditional religious support of work and
frugality.

The Savings Division continued to make its own contacts with
the churches in 1919 and received continued support from religious leaders. Cardinal Gibbons of Baltimore issued a public
letter:

In the hard school of war we have learned much that should be of
value to us and to our country in the days of readjustment. We have
learned the necessity of saving. Indeed it was saving that brought us
the victory—the willingness of the people to save money, to save coal,
to save food. The man, woman or child who has learned to spend
wisely and look forward to the future, to lay by something which will
help him in unforseen emergency, is not only helping himself, but is
becoming a better and more useful citizen.
I urge our clergy to promote this campaign by every means in their
power. I urge our good people to give it their heartiest support.[22]

The schools remained the main hope of the Savings Division.
The promotional task was to convert school war drives into
permanent educational programs. Without that conversion,
thrift education would die along with war patriotism. Consider
the state of Ohio, which had sold the most stamps to school
children by largely ignoring education. "We have a selling organization in the schools," Ohio's representative boasted, "not
a thrift teaching organization. We believe that the children are
tired of text books on how to save. We have . . . a selling campaign." During 1919, Ohio continued its merchandising drive,

using the theme of bringing the boys back from Europe and organizing two "Bring 'Em Back Clubs" in every classroom, with boys and girls in rival selling clubs. For classroom graphics, each club's top seller wore a special button, and a huge cardboard double thermometer recorded with red ink lines the rival (boys versus girls) efforts to raise money. Over summer vacation, Ohio had a stamp-selling contest with 25 top prizes ranging from a Westcott Touring car to an Indian Motorcycle to a set of china dinnerware.[23]

Treasury officials believed that the Ohio plan was an extreme one that would soon burn out without lasting results. The division's educational experts recommended instead an effort to incorporate thrift into regular school programs. That campaign secured passage by the National Educational Association conventions of resolutions calling for thrift to become permanent through school banking, thrift day celebrations, and the integration of saving into the curriculum.[24]

School thrift literature (prepared for the Savings Division by Columbia Teacher College professor George D. Strayer) sought a place in the regular school lessons. The major effort, *Thrift in Schools: Outline of a Course of Study for Elementary Schools* (1919), offered specific suggestions for including thrift lessons in the first eight grades. For first and second graders, little talks on the importance of small savings in the use of paper, pencils, books, shoes, clothing, and food were recommended along with simple math problems in which youngsters could calculate the dimes and nickels needed for a 25-cent thrift stamp. History lessons also began early, with negative messages about the pastoral American Indians whose hunting and fishing lifestyle was said to have created indolent males without savings or thoughts of the future. To be a savage, the *Outline* said, meant to be thriftless. The moral history of thrift for third and fourth graders included positive examples of colonial frontier thrift and negative examples of the ancients in which Roman luxury and extravagance were said to have caused the decline of Rome. Biographies of great Americans—from Benjamin Franklin to Herbert Hoover—taught additional lessons of frugality. For English essays, the list of suggested topics included: "The First Time I ever Admired Savings," "Buying on the Installment Plan," "The Man Without a Savings Account," and "History of Savings in Other Countries."[25]

The *Outline* was distributed to teachers as a suggestion, rather than a final proposal, for working thrift into the curriculum. Teachers and textbook publishers were encouraged to prepare their own materials. The Treasury Department even hoped that the Department of Education (a division of the Interior Department) would eventually take over pushing thrift education. The major difficulty with having Education take over the campaign was that its entire budget was an inadequate $60,000 and it therefore had little standing with local schools.[26]

The main hope of the Savings Division may well have become advertising. Young Treasury officials agreed with a *Saturday Evening Post* representative, C. C. Parlin, who said: "You can, by advertising, put over anything that is fundamentally sound." With advertising from Washington, the Savings Division could sell the universal practice of thrift, creating a "panacea" to alleviate more of the evils and ills of the world than any other reform. Of course, wise old savings bankers attempted to throw cold water on the illusion that moral virtue could be sold by advertising. But the young men at the Savings Division were impatient with advice of old bankers.[27]

Savings optimists were quickly disappointed. Affluent funding of the Savings Division lasted only one year after the end of fighting. For 1919, the $3.5 million budget was trimmed by only one-fourth, but then an economy-driven Congress cut it more than three-fourths in 1920—dropping the division down to $1 million dollars and decimating the Washington staff from 108 to 22. The Savings Division was clearly a victim of a general government thrift program that would cut spending back to pre-war levels.[28]

The new Harding administration publicly supported thrift even more strongly than the Democrats had. Harding came to office in 1921 at the depth of the post-war depression. Unemployment was running almost 12 percent and commodity prices were falling back to pre-war levels, but Harding preached frugality and thrift, not spending. He applauded the work of the Savings Division: "In the present economic state of the world, it is necessary for the people to practice economy in expenditures, and sound methods in investments of their savings." And when Samuel Gomper's American Federation of Labor adopted a resolution asking the Treasury to continue offering savings certificates for laboring men, Harding told Treasury Secretary Andrew Mellon, "I think it would be well worthwhile to inaugurate a peace-time thrift campaign. . . . With labor favoring such a movement it seems an opportune time for government to take it up, and I would gladly cooperate."[29]

Secretary Mellon quickly endorsed thrift. He suggested that Harding might issue a public statement or call a national conference on thrift. But Mellon —reflecting the traditional wisdom of a banker born before the Civil War—lacked faith in government use of advertising to change American behavior and pushed no expansion of the small Savings Division. Mellon believed in thrift, but not in marketing the virtue.[30]

Consumer spending had gone from boom to bust after the war. Heavy buying and high prices in 1919 were followed in 1920 by a "buyers' strike" that reduced purchases and drove down prices. In this economic depression, thrift campaigning came under attack from merchants, who saw it as responsible for depressed sales, closed factories, and growing unemployment. In January 1921, New York City businessmen formed a National Prosperity Committee and launched a campaign of their own for spending. Store windows were plastered with posters of Uncle Sam at the throttle of a locomotive: "Full speed ahead! Clear the track for prosperity! Buy what you need now!" The committee denounced thrift, which had "inevitably reduced the living standards of American workingmen to the niggardly requisites of certain immigrants."[31]

The New York City merchants were not alone in opposing thrift. The *New York Times* editorially declared thrift week sermons "irritating" and "wearisome." Bankers with mercantile loans agreed, and so did manufacturers. Henry Ford, the automobile producer who advertised "Buy a Ford and spend the Difference," also lost all sympathy with thrift—even though he had been a Central Committeeman of the War Savings Division. Ford declared thrift and economy pitiable, overworked concepts: "What can be fine about paring the necessities of life to the very quick? We all know 'economical people' who seem to be niggardly about the amount of air they breathe and the amount of appreciation they will allow themselves to give to anything. They shrivel body and soul. Economy is waste: it is waste of the juices of life, the sap of living." Ford advised young men against saving money before they were 40 years old: "Spend your money on yourself, get all the experience you can. Don't try to save money and be a miser."[32]

Bankers may not have fully agreed with Ford, but they too were enemies of the Savings Division. The government director declared that "the banks have gone out of their way constantly since November 11, 1918, to try to do anything they could to embarrass this movement and put it out of business." Although banks might have profited from thrift education, Treasury produced little propaganda after 1919, but instead confined itself largely to selling treasury certificates at a high interest rate (4.5 percent) which lured deposits away from banks and thus reduced their profits. By the summer of 1922, demands from banking associations that the sale of savings certificates be suspended flooded into the Treasury. Most were from the distressed agricultural regions, but even a Pennsylvania country cashier could complain: *"The war is over, and we believe won.* The Federal Government has ceased to operate railroads, merchant ships, and sell Liberty Bonds on the street corners." No excuse existed for the Treasury to continue competing with private banks, especially after President Calvin Coolidge said, "Agriculture and Banking, like all other interests, are not the business of the Government."[33]

Pressure from state representatives and senators forced Secretary Mellon to cease sale of certificates on July 15, 1924, thus ending the Treasury effort to teach thrift to the American public.[34] Thrift education never had a chance in peacetime: So many interests were offended by a government program against buying that the program had long before ceased to have any real support. After 1920, the Savings Division faded from view. In 1923, Commerce Secretary Herbert Hoover was surprised to learn that savings certificates were still for sale. "Do you mean to tell me that the Treasury is still trying to sell savings securities to the people?" he asked.[35]

So the government thrift program died, largely unmourned,

in 1924. In the roaring twenties, spending, consumption, and display were the dominant style. The public school thrift programs were all that remained of the war savings movement. In 1924, New York City still counted 403 school banks with combined deposits of more than $1 million dollars. Nationwide, there were more than 7,000 school banks in urban areas. Thrift had been expanded in the schoolroom, but could it survive in a consumer-driven culture which no longer permitted government sponsorship of thrift?

8

Frugal Immigrants

Closing the door to foreign immigration can be understood as a parable of prosperous Americans objecting to the more frugal and thrifty habits of aliens. The story began in California, a state which lacked traditional republican commitment to the virtues of self-denial. Populated by young fortune-hunting bachelors in search of golden nuggets, California was never a model of self-restraint: gambling, drunkenness, and licentiousness were typical Golden State behavior. Rowdy Californians sought to exclude Chinese laborers because they consumed less, worked for smaller wages, and threatened to lower the California standard of living. American acceptance of this standard of living argument—which permitted Chinese laborers to be barred from America and led to immigration barriers against aliens in general—marked the American shift away from a thrift society.

Civilized eastern states had initially welcomed immigrants who brought with them the virtues of industry, frugality, and thrift. Criticism of Irish immigrants, the first unwanted aliens in the new republic, had focused on their supposed lack of these virtues. Protestants combined an intolerance of Catholicism with strong objections to the alcoholism, indolence, and pauperism found among the immigrants of the 1840s and 1850s. To be sure, nativists exaggerated in accusing all Irish of lacking traits identified with the Protestant ethic, but certainly Irish immigrants included many "thriftless poor" who filled streets with beggars and the almshouses with paupers. To spare citizens the cost of Irish welfare, as well as the political dangers of enfranchising a people untrained in freedom, nativists agitated to prohibit foreign paupers from entering America and to repeal naturalization laws which permitted aliens to become citizens after five years of residence in America.[1]

Nativist Protestantism provided the moralistic language used by the House Foreign Affairs Committee when it recommended legislation that might prohibit the admission of foreign paupers and criminals. The committee declared that continued American freedom and prosperity depended "on religion and morals, industry and frugality." Crime and pauperism threatened the republic, they said, pointing to the Irish who led the lists of arrested drunks, paupers, and criminals. Testimony published by the committee was even more stereotypical in separating Irish immigrants from native Americans. "The native citizen will not go to the almshouse," a poorhouse director said, "unless his circumstances admit of no improvement; while, on the contrary, an Irishman wants to go there whenever his toe aches."[2]

German immigrants ranked a distant second on arrest and pauper lists, but still Americans worried that these new immigrants of the 1840s might be less virtuous than the old Pennsylvania Germans, who were "frugal, careful of their property, and highly industrious." Germans had earned the reputation of being the best farmers in America. Still, New York City leaders of the 1840s were distressed by the squatter colony of German ragpickers who lived on "Dutch Hill" (Thirty-Ninth Street at First Avenue), surrounded by heaps of rubbish, manure, and "cows, swine, goats and fowls in large numbers." These scavengers were initially suspected of being dirty, lazy, and degraded. But they refused whiskey, drank the milder lager beer, saved their money, and bought western land. By 1857, state authorities concluded approvingly: "Habits of economy and constant application to their wretched business enable nearly all, sooner or later, to accumulate sufficient funds to migrate to the west."[3]

The Protestant ethic provided a major scale for evaluating foreign immigrants in the first half of the nineteenth century. But readings on the scale of virtue were not used to exclude anyone: No immigration restriction was legislated before 1882. Then, however, the testing instrument was reversed, and the failing ethnic group was excluded. Chinese immigrants were excluded not for failing to practice the self-denying virtues but for being more industrious, frugal, and thrifty than native Americans. The exclusion of Orientals might be explained as mere racism, which certainly existed, but it actually reflected a reversal of American values: Consumption had been elevated above thrift. Americans had come to speak of living in comfort rather than plain and adequate living. Immigrants who lived on less and worked for cheaper wages were now perceived as threatening the American standard of living. First applied to the Chinese, the new anti-thrift rules would be expanded to cover all immigrants over the next half century.

The offending Chinese immigration began with the 1849 California gold rush, which lured Asian as well as European fortune hunters. At that time, an Asian could sail to San Francisco more easily than a New Yorker. For centuries, poor but ambitious Chinese had frequently worked outside their empire, seeking wealth which would permit them to return home and live in comfort with their families. Hearing of the California gold rush, many Chinese traveled to California with the dream of finding and saving enough gold to pay their debts and return to China to live in comfort for the remainder of their lives.[4]

In the placer mining camps of the California mountains, the blue-shirted Chinese with their long black pigtails hanging down behind them stood out as very different from Americans. The Chinese were very good miners, perhaps too good, but they worked for cheaper wages and they were foreign. It was not unusual for mining camps to pass resolutions forbidding foreigners to mine. These resolutions excluded Mexicans, Chileans, French, and Chinese, but Asians seemed to draw especially heated opposition. The first anti-Chinese riot occurred in the fall of 1849, when 60 Chinese workers at a British mining camp were driven out by white miners.

In the 1860s, Chinese labor shifted from the mining camps to heavy construction, building the Central Pacific railroad and constructing levees to reclaim the tule swamp lands. There were Chinese farm laborers in the great valleys, and Chinese house servants and manufacturing laborers in the San Francisco Bay area. Although these 50,000 Chinese made up less than 9 percent of California's population, they accounted for 25 percent of wage laborers. As they replaced shoemakers and textile workers in the post–Civil War recession, native craft unions formed an Anti-Coolie Association that defeated the Republican candidate for governor, George Gorham. "I am emphatically opposed," Gorham had declared, "to all attempts to deny the Chinese the right to labor for pay, as I am to the restoration of African slavery whereby black men were compelled to labor without pay."[5] Gorham's defeat taught Republicans that they could no longer win without imitating the Democrat's anti-Chinese propaganda. After 1867, both parties endorsed legislation barring Asians from California.

The Chinese debate never really considered the issue of citizenship for Asians. Federal naturalization law, written in the days of slavery, permitted only "whites" to apply for citizenship, and California used federal law to deny citizenship to the few Chinese who applied. Both Congress and the courts upheld California's racial interpretation of naturalization. The California debate was concerned only with whether Chinese workers should be permitted to come and work. Californian attitudes are amply revealed by the reports of two 1876 San Francisco hearings—the 300-page California State Senate's *Report on Chinese Immigration* and the 1,200-page congressional *Report of the Joint Special Committee to Investigate Chinese Immigration*.

California senators insisted that eastern critics were wrong in denouncing the anti-Coolie movement as merely a crusade against the virtues of industry and economy. The real issue was the American standard of living. The Chinese lived on virtually nothing and saved their money to export to China. The frugal diet of a Chinese laborer cost 15 cents a day, but white laborers could not live like "vermin." The American worker supported a wife, two children, school, church, and culture—requiring $2.50 a day for expenses. The state report said:

Our laborers require meat and bread, which have been considered by us as necessary to that mental and bodily strength which is important in the citizen of a Republic, while the Chinese require only rice, dried fish, tea, and a few simple vegetables. The cost of sustenance to the whites is four-fold greater than that of the Chinese. The Chinese are, therefore, able to underbid the whites in every kind of labor. They can be hired in masses; they can be managed and controlled like unthinking slaves. The Chinese have monopolized the laundry business, cigar making, the manufacture of slippers, sewing, domestic service, harvesting, fruit gathering, railroad building, placer mining, fishing, the manufacturer of silk and wool, and many other occupations.[6]

But California's state senators focused less on the issue of cheap alien labor than on the evils of San Francisco's Chinatown. They sought to demonstrate that the Chinese were the most morally debased race on earth, that virtually all of their pagan women were enslaved prostitutes who spread opium addiction, syphilis, and gonorrhea—and thereby endangered the health and morals of all Americans. Threatened with pestilence, licentiousness, and slave wages caused by the hordes of incoming Mongolians, California whites would surely act in self-preservation and resort to "riot and insurrection," the state politicians said, if Congress did not put an end to Chinese immigration.[7]

When the Joint Committee to Investigate Chinese Immigration met in San Francisco in the fall of 1876, its 130 witnesses were almost evenly divided over the Chinese presence in California. Christian missionaries, railroad capitalists, and large farmers were enthusiastic about Chinese virtues. The Chinese, they said, were the first people to be treated as "criminal and objectionable" because they were "reliable, industrious, or economical." Good farm labor was impossible to find among California's white laborers, who were characterized as "bummers" and alcoholics by one witness, William W. Hollister, who owned 75,000 acres. Lazy, shiftless Americans could not be employed for less than $30 a month, while the reliable, patient Chinese would work for $15 to $25 a month—only slightly more than the prevailing $14 a month for farm labor in the eastern United States. Without Chinese labor, the big farmers said, California agriculture could not prosper.[8]

Reverend Augustus W. Loomis, a Presbyterian missionary who had preached in China, testified to the virtuous rural origins of the immigrants. According to Loomis, most had been "reared in the country, trained to habits of industry and economy and frugality, and accustomed to hear the proverbs of the sages quoted constantly." In California, they were proving their ability by following the Horatio Alger climb from rags to respectability. They came as poor young men, "went to work as house servants, gardeners, or whatever they could find to do, saved their wages and put it out at interest, and when an opportunity occurred for going into business, borrowed from their young friends.... There are innumerable little savings and loan societies among them, companies from five to twenty members.... These industrious and careful boys from China are laying foundations for solid fortunes."[9]

A construction contractor for the Central Pacific, Charles Crocker, testified that the transcontinental railroad could not have been constructed in California without the 10,000 Chinese who accepted the hardest and most difficult labor for $26 a month. Crocker had been unable to hire enough whites at $30 a month plus board, so he had been delighted with his Chinese experiment, which cost the railroad one-third less and provided a sober work force. According to Crocker, the hue and cry against the Chinese was just a wrongheaded repetition of earlier nativist action against the Irish. The anti-Coolie crusade was no more correct than the anti-Irish riot in which he had participated as a boy in Troy, New York.[10]

Although capitalist friends of the Chinese made up half of the committee's witnesses, they represented only a small, defensive minority of Californians. Anti-Chinese hostility had grown increasingly violent in the past two decades. Describing the violent shift against Chinese in San Francisco, a local businessman said, "In 1852 the Chinamen were allowed to turn out and celebrate the Fourth of July, and it was considered a happy thing. In 1862 they would have been mobbed. In 1872 they would have been burned at the stake." Violence now threatened not only the Chinese, but their supporters as well. According to one attorney, Californians no longer permitted freedom of expression about the Chinese: "The friends of the Chinese have been afraid of having their houses burned down. They are afraid of being assaulted and defamed, and having their business injured."[11]

California public opinion had defined the Asian question as a war between the rich and the poor. Chinese labor made "the rich richer and the poor poorer," according to an editor of the *Los Angeles Herald*. Sinophobes argued that the Chinese degraded white labor by creating a tiny aristocracy at the capitalist top and a mass of serfs at the bottom. Rather than have a few rich farmers with 75,000 acres each, California nativists would break the land into small farms of 320 acres owned by an elevated class of white families.[12]

The committee majority, led by California Senator A. A. Sargent, accepted the cheap labor thesis: The Chinese presence was "ruinous to our laboring classes, promotive of caste, and dangerous to free institutions." California needed good white labor, not Oriental slaves, the majority agreed. The Pacific coast must not be Mongolianized by pagans who had too little brain power to be capable of democratic government. Unless checked, the filthy, corrupting Chinese morals might even spread pestilence to eastern cities and make them uninhabitable.[13]

Only the dying Senator Oliver P. Morton issued a strong dissent from the committee's report. Morton, who had fought against slavery, insisted that America must not reassert prejudices against other races and civilizations by excluding the copper-colored people of Asia. America, he said, must make no exceptions to its democratic doctrines of equality and must accept the Chinese as laborers and as citizens. They had come to California as free men, and their labor had not hurt whites, according to Morton. They did work for lower wages while performing the hardest and lowest kinds of labor—constructing railroads, reclaiming the tule lands, and performing every drudgery—but Chinese labor had developed the state and opened new land for homes, work, and jobs. Yes, they had reduced exorbitant California labor costs (which had prevented California agriculture and manufacturing from competing in the world market), but wages had still remained higher than in the rest of the United States; the Chinese had not lowered wages below the national standard. In this free country, Morton insisted, "Labor does not require that a price shall be fixed by law, or that men who live cheaply, and can work for lower wages, shall, for that reason, be kept out of the country."[14]

Congress gave Californians the Exclusion Act of 1882—over objections of Senator Morton and a few other eastern Republicans who recalled that the California arguments of race prejudice and cheap labor had been used against the Irish 40 years earlier, and history had proved those bigoted fears false. The congressional majority departed from the traditional American open-door policy for immigrants and gave California a temporary, ten-year restriction—which, of course, proved to be permanent. Exclusion did nothing to eliminate violence against the 100,000 Chinese laborers who remained. For the rest of the century, ugly riots and massacres dispossessed Chinese immigrants in small towns from San Diego to Seattle.[15]

This legislative rejection of cheap labor created a means of eliminating other immigrants, even the Europeans all congressmen claimed to welcome during the debates of 1882. New threats to the American standard of living were quickly found among these aliens. The Japanese, who had been favorably described during the anti-Coolie debates as willing to imitate American dress, were turned into a working-class threat when their numbers rose to more than 10,000 in the 1890s. Anti-Chinese agitator Denis Kearney turned his San Francisco harangues to the Japanese in 1892, declaring that "foreign shylocks are rushing another breed of Asiatic slaves to fill up the gap made vacant by the Chinese. . . . The Japs Must Go!" By 1900, California trade unions were organizing large-scale protests against the Japanese threat, and the U. S. Industrial Commission's report on immigration (1901) declared the Japanese an "equally menacing" Asian threat.[16]

The frugal and industrious Japanese were said to be driving out not only white labor, but Chinese as well. "They underbid the Chinese in everything," the report declared. They were described as combining untiring industry with disgusting thrift, working from dawn until dark and on holidays. They were the lowest cost producers in small farming and truck gardening, and now they were going into the retail business. Stanford sociologist Edward A. Ross called for legislation keeping out these low-wage foreigners, and American Federation of Labor president

Samuel Gompers declared: "Caucasians are not going to let their standard of living be destroyed by negroes, Chinamen, Japs, or any others."[17]

Restrictionists went from excluding Asians to eliminating European immigration as well, a short step that social scientists, especially the new economists, made easy. Sympathizing with organized labor's efforts to legislate a higher standard of living for the laboring class, the American Economics Association advocated immigration restriction and even offered a $150 prize in 1888 for the best essay on "The Evil Effects of Unrestricted Immigration." Economists pointed to the new immigration from southern and eastern Europe as being racially different. The Italian, the Jew, the Slav, and the Magyar were races that might be impossible to assimilate and Americanize. Professor J. R. Commons worried about the southern Italians who were, he said, "nearly the most illiterate of all immigrants at the present time, the most subservient to superiors, the lowest in their standards of living and at the same time the most industrious and thrifty of all common laborers."[18]

The term *standard of living* meant more than a mere style of consumption. Social scientists wrote chapters and even books on the standard of living because they used the term in a Malthusian sense, meaning the absolute minimum required before an individual would dare to make the commitment to marriage and a family. Fears of Nordic race suicide lurked behind all discussions of the standard of living. Ever since economist Francis A. Walker had connected the drastic decline in the birthrate of old stock Americans to massive nineteenth-century immigration, social scientists were persuaded that the fertility of old Americans had been impaired by immigration: Forced to compete with immigrants whose standard of living was below that of Americans, Nordic Americans, it was said, chose to avoid marriage or to reduce the number of children they had rather than lower their level of civilization to that of the immigrants.[19]

If Chinese and Japanese immigrants could threaten the American standard of living with their superior thrift and industry, so could these workers from rural Italy who were accustomed to a low standard of consumption. Italian males traveled to America as seasonal labor, saved $1000 from their wages, and then returned to Italy to make down payments on real estate. Each year they returned for a season of work, lived frugally, and saved enough to make their mortgage payments. Even Italian laborers who moved their families to America saved more money than Americans did. Social investigators found that these immigrants were indeed more frugal than Americans. Robert Chapin, for example, reported that 58 percent of Italian-American families in New York City saved, while only 23 percent of old Americans spent less than they earned. Laborers who had once been accused of exploiting America by taking their savings back to Italy were now accused of lowering the standard of living and exploiting their own families. An Italian, it was said, starved his wife and put his fourteen-year-old son to work in a factory to help pay for the family home.[20] How could American labor compete with workers who had such an un-American standard of life?

And what about the east European Jews? Everyone knew from Jacob Riis' *How the Other Half Lives* (1890) that the standard of living of Russian and Polish Jews ranked down with the Chinese.

Thrift is the watchwork of Jewtown, as of its people the world over. It is at once its strength and its fatal weakness, its cardinal virtue and its foul disgrace. Become an overmastering passion with these people who came here in droves from Eastern Europe to escape persecution, from which freedom could be bought only with gold, it has enslaved them in bondage worse than that from which they fled. Money is their God. Life itself is of little value compared with even the leanest bank account. In no other spot does life wear so intensely bald and materialistic an aspect as in Ludlow Street. Over and over again I have met with instances of these Polish and Russian Jews deliberately starving themselves to the point of physical exhaustion, while working night and day at a tremendous pressure to save a little money.[21]

The Jewish thrift ethic was the product of more than a thousand years of urban living. Since the eighth century, Jews had been a city people, supporting themselves by commerce and finance. Jewish immigrants in America saved their money to invest in business or educate their children. By postponing current consumption, they would inevitably be able to live much better in the future. It was charged that Jews cheapened the

American standard of living in their ghetto sweatshops, but the truth was that Jews quickly moved into the middle class and were resented for entering resorts, private schools, colleges, and residential neighborhoods. Jews, unlike the humble rural peasants who predominated among immigrants, pushed for middle-class acceptance. When anti-Semitics charged that Jews cheapened American life, they surely had rising enrollments in Columbia and Harvard in mind rather any competition in the labor market.[22]

What could be done about these thrifty foreigners? In 1907, the Dillingham Commission began an investigation of the immigration question that ended four years later with the conclusion that Americans should protect their standard of living from these "new" immigrants by restrictive legislation. Congressman Dillingham first backed a literacy test, which was adopted in 1917, and then switched to a quota system in 1921 as the most effective way to reduce immigration from southern and eastern Europe. In 1924, Congress debated and shrank quotas even further and totally eliminated Japanese immigration. The issues were not unlike those of the Chinese debate. Industrial corporations favored unrestricted immigration, and so-called patriots sought to stop the "deluge" with arguments of racial inferiority and upholding the American standard of living. "Our standard of living is the highest of any country in the world," the restrictionists boasted, "and we do not want to lower it."[23]

Immigrants had spokesmen of their own in the 1924 congressional debates. Fiorello La Guardia, the Jewish and Italian congressman from New York City, ridiculed the Nordics' superiority pretensions. La Guardia did not deny that his people were frugal; in fact, he delighted in comparing them to people living in the hometowns of his opponents. When Congressman Jimmy Byrnes boasted that his South Carolina district had almost no aliens, La Guardia checked his 1923 Postal Savings Annual Report and declared to the Congress:

"Let me give you a few statistics as proof of the industry and thrift of the alien. The gentleman from South Carolina hails from the city of Aiken and according to the report of the Postmaster General there is not a single solitary depositor in the city of Aiken in the postal savings system of the United States. Today the gentleman from Chattanooga brought out the same point, and we find there are just 22 depositors in the postal savings bank. Mr. Cable comes from Lima, Ohio, and in the city of Lima are just 18 depositors having funds in the Postal Savings System, and the energetic whip, the gentleman from Anderson, Indiana, who made a passionate appeal for restrictive immigration a few days ago, we find that he has just 31 depositors in his city putting their savings with the postal system. Now along comes the gentleman from California . . . and he too refers to these terrible aliens, and in the city of Alturas, California, from whence the gentleman comes, there is just one depositor with $10 deposited, and I bet you a dollar to a doughnut that that $10 comes from some little Greek peanut dealer who has saved a penny at a time. The chairman of the committee, Mr. Johnson, who is given to the country by the citizens of Hoquiam, Washington, boasts of 149 depositors in the postal savings bank, while the champion of restriction, the gentleman from Colorado, Mr. Vaile, coming from Denver, had 1,096 depositors, and knowing Denver as I do, I tell you that if you inspect the list of the depositors making up this 1,096, you will find they are Italians, Jews, and Poles among the foreign population of the city of Denver who make up the list.

Now let us take New York City, my little town with its terrible, tremendous foreign population. When you mention it you gasp and you refer to it as the evil you are going to obliterate. Why my town has 186,086 depositors with a total deposit in Uncle Sam's bank of $56,486,528, out of a total savings in the entire United States of $131,671,300 [applause], and if you take the centers where you have large foreign populations and add them up you will see how much is left in the territories where there is no foreign population and who are hounding their congressmen to pass this vicious law. From an inspection of the list from New York City you will find that it is the humble Jew, Italian, Pole, Russian, and Greek immigrant bringing his savings to Uncle Sam because he trusts him, because he knows him, because he loves him, and because he is here to stay. These savings represent the sweat of their brow, the fruit of their honest labor, their part and contribution to the wealth, greatness, and the welfare of their adopted country.

I am willing to take the savings not only in Uncle Sam's savings bank but the savings banks generally, and show you where you have big foreign populations, you have big savings deposits.[24]

Such evidence of immigrant frugality and thrift would have impressed nineteenth-century Americans. But twentieth-century

Americans were offended by superior savings. A people who enjoyed an ever higher standard of spending feared the more simple requirements of foreigners, and more rapid accumulation of wealth by foreigners posed a threat to the affluent style of living. Americans now declared peasant thrift a niggardly, miserly vice. Sophisticated college professors redefined the old virtue to exclude immigrant behavior. "The Italian immigrant who starves his wife and takes his fourteen-year old boy from school to put him in a factory little knows the meaning of thrift," Professor Roy G. Blakey declared. And Harvard economics professor T. N. Carver agreed: "Thrift does not consist in refusing to spend money or to buy things." Carver even went so far as to say that "the thriftiest people are the people with the highest standard of living." This new academic definition of thrift required only intelligent spending and regarded future desires as comparable with present needs. In the long run, Carver said, the thrifty always spent more because they had more to spend. This Harvard definition never logically excluded immigrants from a thrift defense of their judgements to save and purchase a home, but the professor's emphasis on spending gave comfort to American consumers by permitting them to continue thinking of themselves as virtuous.[25]

Along with labor spokesmen and politicians, college professors worried that children of old Americans might be unable to compete with the new immigrants. The most popular sociologist in America, Edward A. Ross, feared the Anglo-Saxon workers would be displaced by the substandard survival habits of immigrants. "Yankee Jim does not rear as many youngsters as Tonio from Abruzzi," Ross wrote, "because he will not huddle his family into one room, feed them macaroni off a bare board, work his wife barefoot in the field, and keep his children weeding onions instead of in school."[26]

Fear of foreigners rose not from theories about the racial inferiority of non-Nordics, but from a real threat of economic competition posed by more thrifty and industrious people. To reduce that threat, the National Origins Act (1924) cut back the tide from southern and eastern Europe and completely excluded the most virtuous, the Orientals. Journalists and scholars frequently explained that the real objections to Chinese and Japanese were that they "worked harder and lived more simply than the Americans and got ahead of their neighbors through diligence." Hostility to Orientals in California emerged not from a belief in their inferiority, but from their superior "industry, skill and thrift."[27]

A connection surely existed between America's closing the gates to immigrants and the decline in the reputation of the word *thrift* during the twenties. As aliens arrived in increasing numbers and cultural varieties, nativist suspicions focused on race, religion, and especially lower standards of living. Fear of foreign competition merged with a new derision of peasant thrift. Americans had never been the most frugal of peoples, but their republican culture had once promoted saving. Now any reluctance to spend was redefined as a foreign threat to the American standard of living.

9

The Moral Revolution

A cultural war against self-restraint—or Puritanism and Victorianism, as it was called—had triumphed in American intellectual circles by the 1920s, dethroning traditional beliefs that had been accepted folk wisdom throughout thousands of years of scarcity. Old words—*restraint, self-denial, inhibition, hard work, sacrifice,* and *thrift*—that had described ideal human character were now declared obsolescent in the new age of abundance. A new lifestyle of gratification rather than restraint represented the modern wisdom.[1]

In New York's Greenwich Village, an important fashion and literary center, prudential restraint had been dropped in favor of "living for the moment." According to Malcolm Cowley's *Exile's Return*, the Bohemian wisdom of the Village affirmed:

It is stupid to pile up treasures that we can enjoy only in old age, when we have lost the capacity for enjoyment. Better to seize the moment as it comes, to dwell in it intensely, even at the cost of future suffering. Better to live extravagantly.[2]

Village indulgence spread throughout the country, according to Cowley, with the help of business interests that found old habits of industry and thrift inadequate to keep the overbuilt factory wheels turning. Industrial capitalism needed a new ethic that encouraged people to buy. The Village idea of "living for the moment" could be used to promote automobiles, radios, or houses—and enjoying them now without paying until tomorrow. Installment buying required a moral revolution against the Puritan ethic, and that revolt was well underway in H. L. Mencken's essays of contempt for the old culture of restraint.

As the *American Mercury's* intellectual leader, Mencken assaulted every sacred conviction. Writing from the Nietzschean perspective that systems of morality outlive their usefulness, Mencken argued that Christianity's slave morality now created only hypocrisy, repression, and bad art. Puritanism had given America the Ku Klux Klan, prohibition, and a Methodist moral obsession to prohibit all enjoyment and pleasure. Calling for liberation in sex and culture, the *American Mercury* also expressed contempt for the "curse of thrift" which was said to obsess New England into saving bits of string while overlooking the enterprise necessary for industrial expansion in the modern age. Mencken and his *American Mercury* shared a general literary radicalism which rewrote former virtues into vices. Just as British novelist D. H. Lawrence declared the wisdom of Ben Franklin a contemptible bourgeoisie morality, so did Charles Angoff's *A Literary History of the American People* (1931) declare Poor Richard "a colossal misfortune in the United States. . . . Franklin represented the least praiseworthy qualities of the inhabitants of the New World: miserliness [and] fanatical practicality."[3]

The new ethic of permissive affluence, with its rejection of self-restraint, flowed inevitably from an industrial capitalism that produced steadily rising standards of living. Traditional thrift had once been required by the hard struggle for existence: When goods were made at home, human nature resisted the misuse or abandonment of shoes, clothing, furniture, or utensils that could be replaced only by one's own hard labor. On moving to the city, however, people were liberated from frugality by money wages, factory production of consumer goods, and advertising. Purse strings were loosened not only for necessities, but for luxuries and amusements such as theater, vaudeville, moving pictures, and baseball—which older Americans pointed to as evidence of a thriftless generation. In 1910, even the automobile had been regarded as a comfort and a luxury. But the traditional ascetic style, as old as human history, succumbed to manufacturers who turned to advertising when production exceeded consumer's desires. The new advertising promoted buying now—enjoying the luxury without waiting and saving to purchase with cash. Credit and advertising grew up together as twin means of increasing sales. Although limited consumer credit can be traced back to 1807 and the New York furniture company of Cowperthwait and Sons, the mass use of credit began with automobile installment buying before World War I and spread to all household goods in the 1920s.[4]

Advertising had been recognized as indispensable ever since the 1920 buyers' strike, when production had soared beyond demand, and advertising offered the only hope of matching consumption with production. Whereas less than $682 million was spent on advertising before the war, almost $3 billion a year poured into advertising in the 1920s. Of course, advertising men rarely admitted that they were campaigning for self-indulgence, wastefulness, and extravagance. They preferred instead to portray themselves as producers interested only in persuading consumers to loosen their purse strings—or buy on credit—for just one product. But the effect of thousands of images surely undermined thrift. The content of advertisements had changed dramatically after J. Walter Thompson published his survey early in the decade concluding that consumers bought dreams, not products. Ads were transformed from informative product announcements to titillating images of psychic byproducts of owning products. New color images portraying situations of fulfillment (and cautionary scenes of humiliation) promised that enjoyment, beauty, good taste, prestige, and popularity would accompany the purchase of automobile bodies by Fisher or Listerine Antiseptic. Advertisers increasingly treated consumers as an insecure, emotional mass with little taste or intelligence, and—with thousands of images appealing to emotions rather than logic—they contributed to producing a mindless consumerism of extravagance and self-indulgence.[5]

Through newspapers, magazines, billboards, radios, and motion pictures, advertising invaded the countryside as well as the city—pushing new ideas, habits, and tastes. Provincial customs weakened under assault from the new industry of promotion, which even gained the approval of the dour president from thrifty New England, Calvin Coolidge. Coolidge commended advertising: "It makes new thoughts, new desires and new actions. . . . It is the most potent influence in adopting and changing the habits and modes of life, affecting what we eat, what we wear, and the work and play of the whole nation."[6]

Experts in the new field of home economics accommodated the new advertising by abandoning frugality advice and embracing the idea of "wise spending." This frugality-versus-comfort issue had been debated among budget experts before the war, with comfort being advocated by *Good Housekeeping* editor Martha B. Bruere, who denounced saving as the "most serious financial mistake." If families saved 12 percent of their income, she wrote in *Increasing Home Efficiency* (1912), they "cut off $300 a year from their pleasure and usefulness." Saving money was viewed as a vice by the new generation of consumer advocates. "Now saving for its own sake isn't an inherent trait in any normal being—praise be!" Bruere said. "Nobody ought to enjoy doing without things, else we should become a race of misers, each sitting on his little separate store of gold."[7]

But Bruere stood outside the professional American Home Economics Association, and her opinions were ignored by most family budgeting professionals, who professed loyalty instead to their prudential founding mother, Ellen H. Richards. The budget advice of Mary Hinman Abel, the 1920s editor of the *Journal of Home Economics*, continued traditional support of frugality and thrift. In *Successful Family Life on the Moderate Income* (1921), Abel applauded a cashier's family who saved 29 percent of the husband's salary, and sharply criticized the wife of a packinghouse manager, whose expensive pleasures—society, entertaining, and vacations—permitted only 3 percent savings. "Her blindness to the future and her determination to have diversion at any cost has made them live beyond their means and rendered savings impossible," Abel declared. But even Mary Abel redefined thrift in her *Journal of Home Economics* to mean not saving but "wise spending of money."[8] Home economics—which focused on instructing the housewife how to feed her family, furnish her home, do her laundry, and otherwise conduct her daily life—taught spending rather than saving. Educating women about the new, labor-saving electric washing machine, dishwasher, refrigerator, and vacuum cleaner stimulated buying, not peasant frugality.

Breaking even more sharply from the frugality tradition were C. W. Taber's *The Business of the Household* (1922) and Christine Frederick's *Efficient Housekeeping or Household Engineering* (1925). These volumes cautioned against "expensive" saving at the price of sacrificing "comfort" and "personal growth and value to the community." Taber urged spending, insisting that "miserliness is despicable; hoarding is vulgar; both are selfish, fatal to character and a danger to the community and nation." Housewives who practiced self-denial and "sordid economizing" surely suffered a "wilting of worthy ambition, the dwarfing of soul and the stunting of the mind and body."[9] The discipline of home economics promoted efficiency and consumer education, not frugality and savings.

While capitalism, advertising, and consumer education were undermining thrift with pressures to buy, the intellectual perspective of socialism was also eroding the practice of frugality by condemning saving as a bourgeois virtue. Socialists were few in number—their candidate, Eugene Debs, won only 6 percent of the 1912 presidential vote—but their influence went far beyond their numbers and persuaded social workers to reject the previous century's belief in temperance, frugality, and industry as the remedies for poverty. Jane Addams, founder of Hull House and a leader in the new field of full-time social work, attributed her conversion from middle-class moralism to a socialist tailor who persuaded her that thrift was impossible for a workingman earning only eight dollars a week. Her tailor insisted that "it would be criminal not to spend every penny of this amount upon food and shelter." The tailor put faith in his children and the social revolution to support him in his old age, not savings or capitalism. Jane Addams agreed that the old "inadequate individual virtues" must give way to new social virtues. It was true, she said, that "the benevolent individual of fifty years ago honestly believed that industry and self-denial in youth would result in comfortable possessions for old age," but modern America required labor unions and the general welfare state rather than Victorian individualism. Jane Addams's reform ideas were so generally accepted in intellectual circles that *The Nation* could say in 1913 that Americans habitually held the Victorian age in "contempt" and that an interest in social reform had led to a belittling of the part played by the individual for himself.[10]

Where was psychology in this shift away from individual character? College teaching had changed dramatically after the escape from moral philosophy. For years, college presidents had the study of the mind tied to ethics and controlled by clergymen who taught that although God had created man with psychological needs and desires, Christianity and moral science defined the limits within which man might gratify those desires and still fulfill his obligations to God and society. Inevitably, however, the moral philosophers lost out to science when psychologists deserted them to study man as a mere biological animal. By 1912, educated Americans were reading a new psychology that popularized the notion of man as an instinctual creature who might best shuck cultural repressions and live free of puritan restraint. The fads—from psychoanalysis to glands to behaviorism—all shared a biological view of man devoid of religion. This self-indulgent, narcissistic preoccupation with the individual self ran counter to the moral tradition of emphasizing concern for the community rather than purely personal needs.[11]

A reputable college professor could no longer urge the self-restraint of Christian character as a solution for social problems as J. Laurence Laughlin had in *The Elements of Political Economy* (1887). "Christian character lies at the basis of industrial progress," the University of Chicago professor had written in an effort to restrain workingmen from striking. "The teaching of the value of the unseen and eternal over the seen and present lies at the foundation of saving, which should be sedulously encouraged. Savings-banks, postal savings plans, cooperative banks, building associations, should everywhere be understood and established by the workmen. Each man should learn to set the future above the present, and thereby learn the secret of self-control, foresight, prudence, and savings. This is, in short, the whole problem of Christian character."[12]

The new social science reduced Laughlin's concept of Christian character to mere custom. Conservative as well as radical professors often agreed that America no longer operated by the old individual virtues in the twentieth century. William Graham Sumner, a mugwump-economist-turned-disillusioned-sociologist, offered an evolutionary description of ethical customs as mere relics from the past. Although truthfulness, love, honor, and altruism were still taught by the books and schools, Sumner said they were not practiced in the real world. "That honesty is the best policy is current doctrine," Sumner wrote in *Folkways* (1906), "but not established practice now. Among ourselves now, in politics, finance, and industry, we see the man-who-can-do-things elevated to a social hero whose success overrides all other considerations." Although he grieved that moral anarchy developed as individuals were emancipated from traditional morality, the secular social scientist had no hope for a moral solution.[13]

Young social scientists were far more hopeful than Sumner. These reform Darwinists believed that ethics might catch up with the evolution of industry beyond competitive capitalism. The optimistic visions of the British Fabian socialists, and the American scoffers of capitalism—Thorstein Veblen and Charles A. Beard—persuaded young Harold Rugg, in 1920, that the day of capitalism was past and that he, as an educator, should write a series of social science textbooks to help students abandon the institutional and moral codes of capitalism for the new cooperative society required by technological evolution. Professor Rugg reflected the intellectual radicalism of his social science reading, Greenwich Village bohemianism, and the Columbia Teachers College discussion group where petit bourgeois virtues were dismissed as a cultural lag.[14]

Even in the Protestant establishment, the old self-denying virtues were under attack. In accordance with psychology and the other social sciences, ministers shifted away from preaching self-restraint. Sermons were no longer filled with denunciations of the self and sinful rebellion against God through self-centeredness. For an affluent, upper-class congregation who no longer believed in a literal interpretation of the Bible, Reverend Harry Emerson Fosdick, the influential pastor of the interdenominational Riverside Church in New York, turned preaching into personal counseling on a group scale. Having experienced an emotional breakdown as a seminary student, Fosdick had a personal interest in mental hygiene and wanted to use psychology to heal pain. He turned his preaching into therapy for his congregation, urging them to use faith to overcome depression, anxiety, and fear. According to Fosdick, individuals should accept themselves and learn the joys of self-realization. Affluent Americans needed a comfortable religion to support their self-realization, and Fosdick became their positive thinker, helping them achieve peace of mind by ignoring conscience and great self-expectations. Religion, which had once warred against evil and the self, now warred against guilt, anxiety, and self-doubt. To be sure, Reverend Fosdick opposed Sigmund Freud, hedonism, and unrestrained self-indulgence, but his permissive message brought comfort to those who would have been repelled by a harsh Calvinist or Wesleyan condemnation of the sinful self. His radio sermons were said to have persuaded a large number of liberal Protestant clergymen to refashion their sermons in the image of counseling sessions.[15]

Faith in hard truths from the age of scarcity had faded amid the prosperity of the twenties. "We are living in the midst of that vast dissolution of ancient habits," Walter Lippmann observed in *A Preface to Morals* (1929). The culture—schools, pulpit, and press—no longer pressed the importance of foresight and savings upon the young. The National Education Association had abolished its Committee on Thrift in 1925, and sales of Horatio Alger novels had declined so sharply that in 1926 the publisher ceased to reprint these nineteenth-century celebrations of industry, frugality, and thrift.[16]

Character and morality were no longer required for success. Public morality had broken from the old-style inspirational oration that had always restrained the self. Even Russell H. Conwell's famous nineteenth-century oration, "Acres of Diamonds"—with its dramatic assertion, "I say you ought to be rich; you have no right to be poor"—actually put public morality first. The Baptist minister explained that wealth should be acquired only for doing good to other people, that greatness "really consists in doing great deeds with little means. . . . He who can give to this city better streets and better sidewalks, better schools and more colleges, more happiness and more civilization, more of God, he will be great anywhere."[17] Popular speakers of the 1920s could no longer be expected to speak from within religious restraints. The amoral orator of the new success ethic, Dale Carnegie, sold a smile-and-con-your-way-to-success speech to New York businessmen. Carnegie laughed at hard work and thrift, insisting instead that manipulation, flattery, and telling a man what he wanted to hear were the new tools for winning in a bureaucratic age. Personality, style, and psychology—rather than character and morality—made up Carnegie's modern message of pursuing self-interest (which he later repackaged as a book, *How to Win Friends and Influence People*).[18] In the popular culture, success had little to do with character and morality.

Certainly, islands of belief in the old values still existed; the prohibition amendment remained in force with the support of rural and small town values. But in advertising, psychology, literature, and religion, the culture of self-restraint had lost its dominance.

10

The Perils of Thrift

The stock market crash of 1929 and the ensuing Great Depression sealed the fate of thrift in the intellectual community. Massive unemployment, idle factories, and closed banks were evidence that individual self-reliance no longer worked. In the debate for a new economic consensus, thrift was without important defenders; its natural allies, bankers, had been toppled and discredited by the depression.

By 1933, more than five thousand banks had shut down without repaying depositors. Even the giant mortgage company organized by S. W. Straus, founder of the American Society for Thrift, had been forced into receivership by the New York supreme court. A full 60 percent of its $400 million in real-estate bonds were in default, and the company was accused of fraud for having sold poor investments to unsuspecting investors. Bankers, once thrift heroes, were now ridiculed before the National Education Association for having urged people to deposit money in their banks. They were now considered an evil to be kept away from children.[1]

Teachers now listened less to bankers and more to radicals such as Stuart Chase. The most widely read popularizer of the left, Chase explained that energy and invention had created an economy of abundance, but the thrift habits of capitalism had clogged the financial arteries: "Savings, hoarding, [and] thrift, operate to freeze economic activity. . . . What was once a virtue becomes in these circumstances a vice." Hard work and thrift had to be replaced by consumption created by government ownership of production and distribution. The financial system of capitalism had outlived its usefulness and should be replaced by socialism. No one should pay attention to conservative nonsense about tightening one's belt, economizing, and living within one's means.[2]

Chase's radicalism was shared by Columbia Teachers College professor John Dewey, who had visited the Soviet Union with Chase in 1927. "We are in for some kind of socialism, call it by whatever name we please," Dewey told teachers. Fellow Teachers College radicals challenged the profession: *Dare the School Build a New Social Order?* they asked. Because capitalism had proven itself "cruel and inhuman," would teachers now indoctrinate children in the evils of capitalism and the necessity of social control over "natural resources and all important forms of capital"? The Columbia group—John Dewey, George Counts, Harold Rugg, and William H. Kilpatrick—was politically to the left of Franklin Roosevelt and the New Deal and called on teachers to lead the nation into socialism. Their journal, *The Social Frontier*, proclaimed a general belief of social scientists: "The age of individualism and laissez faire in economy and government is closing and a new age of collectivism is emerging."[3]

The Social Frontier was very specific in denouncing thrift and savings as "insidious, devastating vice[s]." Spending, not saving, kept an economy going. In the opinion of *The Frontier*, educators should point out the "futility" of thrift and the "folly" of investments in a system where only financial experts profited. Because small investors "inevitably" lost money in banks, stocks, bonds, and real estate, a worker was "far better advised to spend just as rapidly as he makes and to use credit to the limit." To teach the virtue of spending, adult education lectures were recommended, and "all propaganda devices should be used to change archaic attitudes toward savings and investments. Children should be taught to spend, not to save, and at least half of them should be instructed how best to mooch their livings from the industrious." If millions of people were paid not to work—but to consume and spend—then economic stagnation would disappear.[4]

The underconsumption case against thrift was no monopoly of Teachers College radicals. Liberals came to believe that spending could be increased without socialism. Even before the Wall Street collapse of 1929, William T. Foster and Waddill Catchings had warned in *The Road to Plenty* (1928) against the dangers of oversaving. When spending collapsed after the Wall Street crash, Foster and Catchings deplored the "riotous savings" that were ruining the economy. Only consumption and spending could restore the wheels of industry and affluent standards of living. In Utah, troubled Mormon banker Marriner S. Eccles read their case for consumption and began to promote government deficit spending in both Utah and Washington. By 1934, Eccles had an appointment on the Federal Reserve Board and was the most important advocate of spending in the Roosevelt administration, which had reluctantly paid for needed welfare programs without believing deficits were part of a necessary recovery program.[5]

Among professional economists, a few embraced deficit spending in the early thirties. In 1933, eleven University of Chicago professors, including Jacob Viner and Paul Douglas, recommended a deliberate policy of deficit spending. But no American economist made the case for spending so well—and with such technical expertise—as British professor John Maynard Keynes.

Keynes was a rebel who, as a young Cambridge graduate, had joined the Bloomsbury circle of young intellectuals in revolt against Victorian moral codes. "We repudiated entirely customary morals, conventions and traditional wisdom. We were, that is to say, in the strict sense of the term, immoralists," Keynes said. "We recognized no moral obligation on us, no inner sanction, to conform or to obey." In rebellion against all virtue, Keynes easily ridiculed moral assumptions in Victorian economics. With the coming of the Great Depression, he gained fame in American economic circles for denouncing thrift as a pernicious practice. According to Keynes, economy might be necessary to bring down prices in inflationary times, but it only made matters worse in a depression. Only moralistic "fools and madmen" worried about traditional principles rather than finding a solution for the present problem. High wages and prices were not the problem; excessive savings was. In his *Treatise* (1930) and *General Theory* (1936), Keynes advocated government intervention to lower interest rates, to redistribute wealth by heavier taxation, and to spend the nation back to prosperity. If economists were to remain relevant, they would have to abandon the old morality of classical economics and think on a general *macro* level of government.[6]

Seeking to revive the energies of capitalism, Keynes killed traditional faith in the virtue of thrift, which had been a prime justification for inequality of wealth. In the traditional view, wealth was not only the reward for savings and thrift, but it was also the engine which made the wheels of industry go; it employed and fed the masses. Keynes demoted thrift from a virtue and a motor of progress to a vice—to be denounced even more than prodigality which, in fact, ought to be applauded in the depression. Ridiculing individual virtue, Keynes rested his macroeconomics instead on the goal of full employment. Whatever restored full employment—spending—should be encouraged. Whatever retarded employment—savings—should be discouraged.

In economics, as well as in psychology and the other social sciences, traditional emphasis on the individual became unacceptable. The old approach—"blaming the individual," as it was phrased—lost out to trusting the state. In the Soviet Union, government socialism had eliminated poverty and wide extremes of income. At home, statistical studies proved that only a minority of poverty cases were actually the result of personal misconduct—laziness and shiftlessness. Most poverty resulted instead from misfortune that was beyond the control of the individual. Certainly, the general economic trouble in the Great Depression was due to overproduction and underconsumption, not a lack of personal savings. So thrift ceased to be a concern of social scientists, and American economists could happily declare the virtue of thrift dead or dying. "Only where the older virtues of thrift are tied into religious beliefs and practices,"

Professor William L. Nunn said, "as in scattered parts of the New England states, in the Mormon areas and in the Dunkard, Mennonite and Amish communities, have they been preserved."[7]

Surely the professor exaggerated. Alienation from thrift seemed more common among intellectuals than the general public. When Robert Lynd's research staff asked Muncie, Indiana residents if the installment buying boom of the twenties and the economic depression of the thirties had changed the public faith in saving, the answer seemed to be no. Of course, the researchers heard complaints that labor and the young were rejecting painful self-denial for a spend-it-if-you-have-it prodigality. The local newspaper objected that welfare programs of the New Deal were ruining the traditional faith. "Our parents and grandparents taught their sons that the good things of life came through work, ability, and saving," the "Middletown" newspaper editorialized in 1935.

Now children are being taught that the less work the better, that one who is without skill has the same right to the fruits of the earth as the man of high intelligence, and that spending for spending's sake alone is virtue and thrift is vice. . . . Is it not about time for the American people to go back to that common sense which for a century and a half has served them well enough to build a nation that is the envy of all others?[8]

Despite all the talk of a moral revolution against thrift, Lynd found that most of Middletown still believed in the traditional virtue. The economic shock of depression seemed to have turned people back to thrift. A carpenter observed: "One of the lasting changes made by the depression is that it has shown people they can't live beyond their earnings. It's taught us frugality." And another said: "We were all damned fools in the 1920s! We thought we had the world by the tail and forgot the old truths that 'a nickel saved is a nickel made!' I'm never again going to get caught the way I was in this crash. From now on I'm going to live within my income and you bet I'll save! I don't know where I will keep my savings, but I'll keep 'em all right."[9]

The depression had certainly tarnished the twenties ideal of burning the candle at both ends. Economic security was now the chief preoccupation of Americans. Traditional concern for thrift and savings returned, along with a new demand for federal social insurance against the specter of poverty and dependence. "We used to assume that if people were industrious and thrifty they could earn enough to support themselves and their families," the editor of the *Journal of Home Economics* conceded. "Now we recognize that willingness and ability to work are not enough to assure one of a job, that whether the factory is to run or not often depends on things far beyond individual or local control, that producing a crop does not always mean making profit out of it, that the most carefully considered investments may fail."[10] Americans supported social insurance against unemployment, sickness, and old age dependency—as well as personal thrift to provide more than the bare minimum of security.

The continued high regard for thrift and savings among insecure Americans may explain the erratic behavior of President Franklin D. Roosevelt. In his 1932 campaign, Roosevelt had attacked Herbert Hoover as a spendthrift: "Any Government, like any family, can for a year spend a little more than it earns. But you and I know that a continuation of that habit means the poorhouse." Roosevelt the politician used traditional rhetoric—balancing budgets, restoring competition, and saving capitalism—while at the same time extending a social-welfare safety net, making structural changes, and spending more than his government collected. Because 70 percent of the voters opposed deficit spending, and only 25 percent were willing to continue spending until prosperity returned, Roosevelt continued to talk of a balanced budget. There is little evidence that Roosevelt ever really converted to a belief in Keynesian economics; he even attempted a balanced federal budget in 1937, a move that threw the economy into another recession. In many respects, the shifty politician was probably closer to his Dutch Calvinist ancestors than to the new macroeconomists.[11]

Although Keynesian economics had not really penetrated the White House or the general public, it had reached the academic community. In the autumn of 1936, it hit with "tidal force," according to John Kenneth Galbraith, and swept along most of the younger professors. It took two more years and the recession of 1938 for the new theory to persuade the older intellectual establishment. During the 1938 recession, New Dealers needed to explain why five years of deficit spending had not brought recovery. Keynes's *General Theory* blamed a flaw in mature capitalism that prevented sufficient investment for full employment. The trouble was (economists could now argue with some theoretical support) that the New Deal had failed to spend enough to overcome the stagnation in capital investment. Seven Harvard economists issued a Keynesian manifesto in the fall of 1938. In December, American Economics Association president Alvin Hansen delivered his radical Keynesian message. Hansen used his forum to call for increased taxation of the rich and massive social programs to cure the economic stagnation that had not responded to the mild pump priming of the Roosevelt administration.[12]

Once established as the dominant theory among Harvard economists, Keynesian ideas were certain to get a hearing within the national government. In 1939, Lauchlin Currie became the first professional economist appointed to the White House as a presidential assistant, and he recommended only reliable Keynesians for further government appointments. The Secretary of Commerce, Harry Hopkins, set up a new division for Keynesians, and the Budget Bureau was transferred from Treasury to the White House. Within a couple of years, Keynesians held prominent government positions—including Alvin Hansen on the National Resources Planning Board and John Kenneth Galbraith at the Office of Price Administration.[13]

With Keynesians holding places of power in the government and universities (and with a significant segment of the business sector accepting Keynesian analysis), the idea that thrift was no virtue trickled down. Of course, traditionalists were still a numerical majority. At Columbia Teachers College, protested one such traditionalist: "The most dangerous suggestion for the long-term economic welfare of the country . . . is that we should stop the discussion and teaching of thrift." But the highest intellectual and political ground had been seized by those who shared the new economic faith that government, not individual, action promised security.[14]

The new historical presentation of the recent past described thrift as a key to what had gone wrong. Students were taught that for more than a hundred years, "Americans had been lectured constantly on the virtue of frugality and thrift." According to Thomas C. Cochran and William Miller's *The Age of Enterprise* (1942), billions in savings had poured into transportation and manufacturing plants, until most of the traditional areas for profitable enterprise had closed as the economy reached maturity by 1914. Savings had mounted faster than new investments, and "the conventions of thrift and frugality impeded the growth of consumer goods industries." American business had collapsed in 1929 from excessive savings. *The Age of Enterprise* told readers that future prosperity depended on government planning and an end to the old days of thrift and laissez faire.[15]

11

The Thriftless Society

The official departure from a thrift culture became evident during World War II. Military needs required cutting domestic spending, but the Roosevelt Administration issued no call for traditional thrift. In fact, all opportunities to propagandize for thrift and saving money were avoided. Government officials now either feared or disdained thrift and refused to use the old methods of financing a war effort. The private virtue had become a vice that government no longer encouraged.

The new rules for war finance had been laid down by John Maynard Keynes's London *Times* articles in November 1939. Keynes understood that nations must move back from the Age of Plenty to the Age of Scarcity. Populations must consume less, permitting enormous war consumption while restraining civilian demand and price inflation. Keynes had no faith in reducing demand by voluntary restraint, by encouraging the instinctual vice of thrift. Voluntary savings would never be adequate, he declared; consumption must instead be restrained by forced savings. The Keynesian solution required government control of savings as well as materials, prices, wages, and capital. Rather than depend on the old-fashioned practice of individual self-restraint and voluntary bond purchases the government should force savings by deducting up to 21 percent of income after taxes.[1]

When American prices began to rise in 1941, the realistic, Keynesian administrators imposed a price freeze and established rationing for necessities in short supply. Central planning reflected Keynesian economic wisdom. Economists, not individual consumers, should make price and market decisions. Luxuries such as automobiles, radios, refrigerators, pleated skirts, and silk stockings were eliminated from production by government decree. By eliminating the free market, the New Deal Office of Price Administration kept inflation down to less than three percent a year until the end of the war.[2]

Federal Reserve Board Chairman Marriner Eccles—and all informed economists—endorsed compulsory savings. Only the Treasury Secretary Henry Morgenthau, Jr.—and the majority of Americans—wanted a voluntary war savings program. Morgenthau, a Dutchess County farmer and neighbor of Franklin Roosevelt, clung to the old economics of balanced budgets and individual choice. He wanted to permit Americans the opportunity to do something voluntarily in the war effort. Voluntarism would be good for morale in a war against totalitarian governments, Morgenthau said. And the President agreed with him, as did the majority of voters. "Everybody else is against it," Roosevelt said, "but we are going to do it."[3]

While Roosevelt and Morgenthau conducted a voluntary war savings program, they took care to avoid further offending the Keynesians. They never advocated thrift as a means of selling war bonds. Both had been born to inherited wealth and had never lived with the frugality and thrift of a scarcity society. President Roosevelt never accused Americans of extravagance; he never preached thrift. In his fireside chats, the President spoke of patriotism when he promoted war bonds. Buy bonds to defend democracy and redeem civilization from the enemy, Roosevelt said. "Every dollar that you invest in the . . . War Loan is your personal message of defiance to . . . the ruthless savages of Germany and Japan." Moreover, bond purchases would hold down inflation and prevent a post-war depression. The President never advocated bonds as means of instilling character and virtue.[4]

Secretary Morgenthau occasionally slipped into the old moralistic language: "It's not only smart to be thrifty, but our future depends upon it." But he, too, saw the object of savings bonds as giving "every American a sense of direct participation in the financing of national defense." His Treasury Department never used thrift language in its pamphlets, but instead packaged war savings as patriotism—"Back the Attack," "They Give Their Lives; You Lend Your Money"—and as economic planning. Bonds could prevent runaway inflation by soaking up consumer dollars, thereby restraining price increases during government war spending. Cashing in bonds after the war would replace military spending and thus prevent economic depression. All talk of teaching thrift and moral virtue was avoided because thrift had become a dangerous American habit.[5]

Planners did not want to encourage a habit that would restrain Americans from spending all their war bond savings on consumer goods after the war. Avoiding a post-war crash obsessed planners. How could disaster be avoided when the $250-million-per-day war spending was stopped and the twelve-million-man fighting force came home? During the last years of the war, hundreds of articles and books on the employment question were published.

An important example of planners' hopes for coercing Americans into big spending after the war was Robert R. Nathan's *Mobilizing for Abundance* (1944). The great fear of Keynesian planners such as Nathan was that the abnormally high war savings rate of 24 percent would not only continue into peacetime, but it might even increase, unless the government encouraged spending and discouraged savings. If Americans did not stop believing that thrift was a virtue and spending a vice, then democracy and the free enterprise system would not survive; the economic system ran efficiently only on mass consumption. Government action must raise the incomes of the poor (who were excellent spenders) and tax the wealthy (who habitually saved too much). And Congress must provide bigger and better social security—including health and accident insurance—to discourage personal saving for retirement and misfortune. If Americans wanted to save, sell them government bonds and use the money for superhighways, schools, public power projects, and welfare payments.[6]

Planners need not have worried. Government controls may have compelled Americans to save one-fourth of their disposable income during the war, but savings fell to 5 percent once peace returned. Massive consumer spending brought double-digit inflation—driving prices almost 50 percent higher by 1948. Americans had learned that spending was splendid. In the late forties, installment debt rose from 2 to 5 percent of personal income, then it doubled again to 10 percent by the late 1950s. Consumer credit skyrocketed as the new credit cards, Diners' Club and American Express, encouraged Americans to enjoy now rather than wait. Home economists praised consumer credit for raising living standards of Americans with a "new way of life—buying today, paying later. . . . Installment buying is now a part of our culture. . . . It can no longer be viewed . . . in terms . . . of poor personal management or excessive gratification of needs and desires."[7]

Borrow and spend became the American way during the 1950s. The *New York Times* annually poked fun at the banker's Thrift Week by collecting humorous observations to print in the back of their magazine section: "Thrift is a wonderful virtue, especially in an ancestor"; "Any young man with good health and a poor appetite can save money"; "In the good old days a man who saved his money was called a miser; now he is called a wonder."[8]

To be sure, traditional thrift propaganda continued. Sylvia F. Porter called savings a "must" for any family seeking "security, independence, or the realization of a cherished dream." The McGraw-Hill textbook on consumer education persisted in the hard-sell thrift advocacy that said only thoughtless children and savages didn't save. "The successful man in this world is the one with the ability to save money and to invest it wisely after it has been saved," declared *Your Personal Economics* (1953). "Where you stand 10 years from now—how you stack up as a person and as a member of the community—will depend largely on how consistently you have held on to your money." Also:

"Savage peoples have almost no ability to look ahead. They eat all the game they kill today; then they may nearly starve before they find more. The ability to look ahead—to put off something now for the sake of something better in the future—is the mark of the real grownup and of civilized man."[9]

The U. S. Treasury's savings stamp and bond program, begun during World War II, continued with new emphasis on thrift as well as patriotism. As the Eisenhower administration reduced the public debt during the 1950s, thrift was promoted as a virtue for both the nation and the individual. The words *frugality*, *Scotch*, and *savings*—and the name Benjamin Franklin—were again in good repute at the Treasury. A 1958 pamphlet, "In Family Thrift the Lady Leads," recommended Franklin's words: "Frugality is an enriching virtue. . . . I was once lucky enough to find it in a wife who thereby became a fortune to me." School-children were still taught frugality and thrift by a federal program.[10]

Obviously, American children still heard a good deal about thrift in the 1950s. There were elementary school banking operations in the Northeast and other urban centers, and many textbooks and teachers continued to have favorable things to say about thrift. The great majority of children told pollsters that they heard "a great deal" about thrift at school and home.[11]

Yet college professors were teaching that American character had changed in the age of affluence. A new other-directed personality had replaced the stern, inner-directed American, according to David Riesman in *The Lonely Crowd* (1950). The old scarcity psychology had created inner-directed puritan types so indoctrinated with the virtues of industry, frugality, and thrift that they succeeded in building an industrial, urban civilization. Modern affluence, on the other hand, had produced a new abundance psychology—Americans whose wasteful leisure consumed the surplus created by the old-style capitalists. According to Riesman, these other-directed Americans were popularity seekers without internal gyroscopes who followed the style of their peers and always felt anxious that they might not be properly adjusted to the group. Their insecurities made them great consumers and spenders.[12]

Sociologist C. Wright Mills observed that the middle-class ethic had become a relic in the 1950s, replaced by a leisure ethic. Employees no longer lived to work and save for the future, but to spend and enjoy now. Work represented the dreariest part of life, necessary only to support the gayest part—consumption during leisure hours. The machinery of advertising and amusement helped to preoccupy Americans with pleasure as the workday shrank to six or seven hours. Television, golf, skiing, and vacations became national habits. Americans now lived to spend, to go on holiday. Their idols were no longer the business, professional, and political figures, but leisure stars from movies, athletics, and music. Work had become alienating, boring, restraining, and a grind, whereas leisure provided meaning, glamour, thrills, and prestige.[13]

History textbooks credited American post-war prosperity to massive consumer and government spending. Hofstadter, Miller, and Aaron's *The American Republic* (1959) explained that Americans had been "aching to spend" their $140 billion of war savings and another $140 billion of borrowed money. Even though credit had increased the cost of a new automobile by one-third, installment purchasing became so common that a cash buyer was "likely to be condemned as un-American and kept at the bottom of the waiting list." Credit grew so popular that retail stores earned more profit from interest charges than from the price mark-ups of the goods themselves. And easy credit had government encouragement: Federal income tax allowed a 100 percent deduction for interest paid. With government encouragement of credit and heavy federal spending for highways and national defense, *The American Republic* taught, the post-war economy "purred."[14]

The generation educated after World War II read *Economics*, the best-selling college text by Paul A. Samuelson. The first edition in 1948 explained that high consumption brought health to a nation while thrift could be a social vice. Spoofing the old virtue, the Keynesian professor wrote: "In kindergarten we were all taught that thrift is *always* a good thing. Benjamin Franklin's 'Poor Richard's Almanac' never tired of preaching the doctrine of saving." The old truth applied only to primitive agricultural communities; in a modern commercial depression, the belt tightening of traditional frugality worsened the vicious deflationary spiral. Clearly, Samuelson concluded, "private prudence may be social folly."[15]

So college students in the 1950s learned how to avoid an economic depression, and they generally held in contempt President Dwight D. Eisenhower's refusal to fully accept the new economics. The post–Korean-war recession of 1954 worried Eisenhower, who wanted to avoid being labeled a "do-nothing Herbert Hoover." Eisenhower planned to step up federal spending if unemployment rose above 5.5 percent, but the mild recession cured itself. In the deeper recession of 1958, when unemployment hit seven percent and Democrats called for a tax cut as well as massive public works, Ike resisted all pressure to spend, although he admitted: "I realize that to be conservative in this situation can get me tagged as an unsympathetic, reactionary fossil." Commitment to the old virtues of thrift and a balanced budget tarnished Eisenhower's reputation among intellectuals of the fifties.[16]

Economists and consumers no longer agreed with Adam Smith that thrift had roots in human nature. A modern savings theory, spelled out by professor Franco Modigliani, cut all connections with thrift and virtue. Individuals saved only when they had extra money and a specific need for savings. In this life-cycle theory, middle-aged people saved for retirement and then spent to die with zero savings. Economic theory now assumed that Americans were perfectly rational consumers. No thrifty misers existed to enjoy the power of accumulated money; we were spenders all.

The problem in the age of affluence, according to Keynesian economists, was how best to spend all our wealth. Because traditional economic ideas inherited from the world of poverty and scarcity were irrelevant, John Kenneth Galbraith's best-selling *The Affluent Society* (1958) advised the nation to direct its attention away from the production and toward the distribution of wealth. Let government tax and spend for the general welfare—roads, schools, pollution control, and the elimination of poverty. We were rich enough to provide more leisure and culture now that the painful old days of capitalism—with its mindless concern for balanced budgets and the production of wealth—had been written off as obsolescent.[17]

By the 1950s, the word *thrift* had been eliminated from the American vocabulary. Thrift articles were no longer printed in magazines. Although the word could still be found in *Webster's*, it had disappeared from the encyclopedias. The 1952 *Britannica*, in its Adam Smith essay, explained that thrift was now looked upon as a "pernicious practice" by economists who had once been among its arch-advocates. *World Book* preserved its long essay on thrift until the 1960 edition, but then it substituted a short, morally neutral entry—savings.

The moral revolution against Victorian restraint had succeeded so fully by the 1960s that the high ground in education was occupied by those opposed to values indoctrination. The term *values* had come into common use after the 1930s as a substitute for the traditional language of morals and virtues. No teacher had the "right" set of values for modern children, it was said. Values were personal "preferences," and students should choose those they liked best. Home economists actually rejected traditional thrift values even before giving students a choice. "The old Puritan ethic of thrift and frugality no longer applied to family behavior in the United States in this era of abundance," wrote Irene Oppenheim in *Management of the Modern Home* (1972). None of Ms. Oppenheim's budget families saved, she said, because the modern feeling assumed that the family should "be committed to getting as much as we can now." Home economists taught that the new attitude was good for economy, whereas the old attitude, "which grew out of the earlier Judaeo-Christian heritage, was an outgrowth of an economy of scarcity where food and other goods were hard to obtain."[18]

While home economists were still writing against puritanism, youth of the 1960s were rebelling against New Deal liberalism. Students who had grown up in the age of affluence could not rebel against a thrift culture they had never known, so when they rejected Lyndon Johnson's Vietnam War, they also rejected the liberal corporate state—with its mindless consumerism, boring bureaucracy, and souless alienation from life and beauty. So far removed were hippies and Woodstock from the culture of thrift that the affirmation of faith in their countervalues, *The Greening of America* by Charles A. Reich, did not even acknowledge that frugality had ever existed. This Yale law professor, whose consciousness had been raised by the 1967 "summer of love" in Berkeley, omitted thrift from his description of the creed of early American capitalists. Those "supersquare primitives of Con I," according to Reich, had believed only in individual character, morality, and hard work. The Horatio Alger types were then replaced by the "New Deal Con II," which turned Americans into uptight prisoners of the corporate state. In the name of public interest, the welfare state had turned Americans into mindless robots who were required to do their duty for the state and the corporation. But salvation was at hand because the young had dropped out and developed "Consciousness III,"which led them to wear groovy beads and bell-bottoms, smoke pot, love people, and eat natural peanut butter. Reich assured his readers that the liberated consciousness would erode the oppressive corporate state.

Distrusting reason and logic, Reich's flower children listened to their appetites and feelings. They were detached from both the culture of restraint and the culture of affluence. Of course, flower children were only partially representative of their generation, but they clearly illustrated a collapse of the old self-restraint ethic among middle-class students at elite universities.

Modern youth had learned self-indulgence. Most believed high spending rather than high saving was good for the economy and for themselves. By 1974, almost three out of four youngsters thought that spending rather than thrift was most beneficial for the economy. According to Lester Rand Youth Polls young people spent their money and "easily justified their overall wastefulness by claiming that it contributes to greater consumption and therefore benefits the economy as a whole."[19]

American youth rarely, if ever, heard thrift discussed at school or home. The traditional parental instructions—"A penny saved is a penny earned," and "Save for a rainy day"—had been replaced by almost $100 million of television advertising that urged little ones to spend for instant gratification. Watching twenty-five hours of television a week, children absorbed (especially on Saturday mornings) 200 advertising messages crafted for them. And youngsters reacted as they were instructed. Of course, four-year-olds had some trouble getting to stores to spend more than 45 percent of their allowances, but twelve-year-olds became almost perfect consumers. By the 1980s, they spent 99.6 percent of their income, saving only 23 cents of their $5.49 average weekly allowance, and using the rest for sweets, snacks, toys, games, fun machines, movies, and entertainment. The consuming child had become typical in all social classes, with lower- and middle-class children spending proportionally more than upper-class children. The child who saved was out of step with playmates, as well as with most American adults.[20]

A full 20 percent of American families had no net worth beyond their consumer goods. Disregarding real estate, 55 percent of families had no net worth. Most Americans, in other words, saved no money except what they put into their homes and consumer goods. Only a minority held financial assets, contributing to the national investment funds. Americans distinguished themselves as debtors, not lenders. The percentage of families with consumer installment debt rose from 53 to 59 percent between 1970 and 1986. And dollar amount of that debt increased from 100 billion to 552 billion during that same period.[21]

The few conservative voices who spoke for economy were outside the confidant mainstream that believed affluent consumption could continue forever. A reader would have to turn to the conservative *U. S. News and World Report* for a traditional editorial quoting a poem by Conrad Aiken:

> All lovely things will have an ending,
> All lovely things will fade and die,
> And youth, that's now so bravely spending,
> Will beg a penny by and by.[22]

12

The Politics of Debtor America

The erosion of faith in frugality, thrift, and savings was so complete as America made the shift from creditor to debtor nation in the 1980s that President Ronald Reagan issued no call for a return to individual thrift, nor did he really try to balance the federal budget. Reagan came to the presidency before the public debt had reached a trillion dollars, but his administration more than doubled that figure by adding another 1.5 trillion dollars of deficit. Despite the pretense of traditional conservative values, neither Reagan nor his Republican advisers believed in frugality and thrift. Instead, they planned to spend their way to prosperity. Patriotic appeals for sacrifice and austerity were no longer considered effective Republican techniques for governing. The *Washington Monthly* could survey the capitol city and conclude: "No one here is proposing that we once again celebrate individual thrift as a social virtue.[1]

Everyone had become values-neutral—economists, capitalists, and politicians. President Reagan might use the old moralistic language when speaking of foreign policy, he might call the Soviet Union an "evil empire"—but he never criticized personal economic behavior. A believer in the modern value relativism that no one need feel bad about oneself, Reagan insisted that economic troubles were not the fault of individuals but of government. And yet he never subjected government to any economic discipline. Despite much talk of a balanced budget, he never resisted spending more than the Internal Revenue Service collected. The President differed with liberals only on how best to unbalance the budget—tax cuts rather than spending programs—if doubling the defense budget can be considered a Reagan spending exception. Liberal Keynesians maintained that the country badly needed more government spending, but Reagan and the business establishment pushed instead for tax cuts. The President reflected the new business Keynesianism that dated back to the Kennedy tax cut.[2]

In 1960, America had elected its first president who was not a pre-Keynesian. John A. Kennedy had little interest in economic theory. He had grown up in the post-Keynesian world and was therefore less attached to the old belief in a balanced budget. When a business slowdown was followed by a stock market slump in 1962, he was easily persuaded of the merits of a quick tax cut. Of course his advisers called for reducing taxes: Conventional economic wisdom held that more money in consumers pockets would prevent a sluggish economy from turning into a depression. Only John Kenneth Galbraith protested that a tax cut rather than more government spending was reactionary Keynesianism. Walter Heller, Paul Samuelson, and the majority of economists advised a quick tax cut. Even so, Kennedy resisted the idea until business joined the lobby for a tax slash and a budget deficit. All the business groups—the National Association of Manufacturers, the U. S. Chamber of Commerce, and the Committee for Economic Development—put tax reduction high on their agendas. When Kennedy first proposed reducing federal taxes before the wealthy Economic Club of New York City, the capitalists' warm applause convinced the president that budget deficits were a popular technique for getting the country moving again.[3]

After Kennedy's assassination, Lyndon Johnson carried out the tax cut, and the cash multiplier worked as predicted. Both the economy and tax revenues grew. Upon entering the Vietnam War in 1965 for a major effort, Johnson continued the no-pain financing, asking for no taxes, no rationing, no victory bonds, no sacrifice from anyone except young draftees. The affluent young naturally rebelled against sacrifice in a struggle with so little purpose. And the war economy naturally created a textbook example of government-created inflation. When massive military purchasing competed in the civilian market for leather, boots, labor, and other items, prices and wages rose. By 1968, inflation had accelerated from 2 to 4.5 percent.

The Republican administration of Richard Nixon promised to cut government spending, and so it did until reelection time. To get himself reelected, Nixon announced himself a Keynesian and pumped up the economy, which touched off another spiral of inflation. With the help of the OPEC oil embargo, inflation had soared to double digits—11 percent—by 1974, terrifying American savers and threatening millions who lived on fixed incomes.

After Watergate, the Ford administration reapplied the old remedy for inflation—tight monetary and fiscal policies—and threw the economy into recession. Penn Central, New York City, and much of the housing industry went bankrupt. The Ford shock of recession cut inflation by half, but it probably elected Democrat Jimmy Carter to the White House.[4]

The Vietnam War, which drove the American economy into its binge of inflation and recession, also killed off the Treasury Department's savings stamp program. Throughout the 1960s, the program had continued to reach thrift and citizenship to America's schoolchildren by promoting savings as "an important part of our heritage." But "The Stamp of a Good Citizen" who backed "our men in Vietnam" inevitably became controversial when public opinion turned against the war. When inflation soared beyond modest stamp and bond interest, the stamps also became bad investments, and participation in the federal school savings program declined. On February 2, 1970, President Nixon's Treasury Secretary announced that the federal government had dropped its school savings stamp.[5]

Inflation also closed school banking programs when their thrift bank sponsors were caught by state regulations that held maximum bank interest to 5.5 percent while money market funds were free to offer 15 percent in search of deposits. Thrift banks could no longer give schoolchildren a good deal when they themselves were losing money, and even becoming insolvent, as depositors moved their savings to other financial institutions. So school savings banks were dropped and American children lost their last program of thrift education.[6]

The economy itself was also in trouble. The same economy that had long maintained the highest standard of living in the world no longer produced abundance, and its troubles were not confined to inflation and the energy crisis. America had slipped to fifth place—behind Switzerland, Denmark, West Germany, and Sweden—in terms of per capita income. These countries and Japan (with its standard of living rapidly approaching ours) had less domestic energy that America. Oil prices were clearly not the only problem with the American economy; industrial productivity had also slipped. American output per hour of work—which had increased for more than a hundred years—actually declined. One problem was that Americans had not saved enough to provide the workers entering the labor market with the $50,000 worth of plant and equipment necessary to keep competitive. We had saved too little and bought too few industrial robots. Our consumption had overtaken our production.[7]

Some journals of opinion predicted that the shock of the energy crisis would bring about a permanent change in America's profligate lifestyle. Environmentalists claimed that the earth had taught us the necessity of a return to moral virtues of the simple life. Advertising agencies even promoted less buying, less heating, and less driving. More than three million Americans took up energy-efficient vegetable gardening and wood-burning stoves. Millions more purchased small, fuel-efficient automobiles. President Carter accepted sacrifice as a necessity and—in the jeremiad tradition—indicted Americans for having strayed from the virtues of our founders. Government could not solve the energy problem; only the people could, by giving up their worship of self-indulgent consumption and returning to traditional values of frugality, mutual aid, and spirituality.[8]

The hedonistic culture laughed at Carter's sermons. Only idealists among the environmentalists were willing to return to frugality. When a second oil shock in 1979—combined with Carter's benevolent efforts to raise the income of farmers, the elderly, and low-wage workers—sent inflation soaring to 12.4 percent by 1980, Ronald Reagan easily deposed Carter. The Republican candidate appeared to be a traditional conservative: he denounced Communism, big government, welfare, taxes, and budget deficits. He won support from the so-called moral majority of organized evangelical Christians by opposing court decisions on abortion, prayer, and school busing. But Reagan only campaigned against big government, not for a restoration of the old individual virtues. He was no Cato the Censor. As California governor, he had advocated less, then increased the state budget by 122 percent. He never advocated personal frugality or thrift, but rather ridiculed Carter's call for Americans to reduce consumption. Reagan never criticized the moral fiber of Americans, but praised voters and promised to get government "off their backs" and to restore "growth and productivity." Reagan appeared as a romantic, promising that painless prosperity would flow from tax cuts, which would stimulate higher consumption and greater investment, which would in turn balance the budget and pay for the arms build-up.[9]

The President had an economics tutor whose lecture notes promised a rosy scenario of prosperity. Milton Friedman, creator of the "monetarist" school of economic thought at the University of Chicago, had retired to Reagan's California in the 1970s. There the energetic professor began a series of public lectures in 1977 that led to 15 videotaped performances and a public television series. Friedman, a master of the snappy phrase, preached limiting the money supply, cutting congressional spending, and letting the free market solve all our troubles. Ronald Reagan contributed an enthusiastic endorsement for the dust jacket of Friedman's *Free to Choose* (1980), a book that bitterly opposed government taxing for social programs but omitted any advocacy of traditional financial virtues. The index to *Free to Choose* contained no entries under *deficit*, *thrift*, or *savings*.[10] Friedman tutored Reagan away from all traditional concern about consumption and debt. If we could move toward abolishing government, why worry about national deficits?

The President's other favorite economic writer was George Gilder, the author of *Wealth and Poverty* (1981), which illustrated Reagan's departure from traditional conservative values. Gilder agreed that welfare programs were the major evil facing America, but his remedy was less a restoration of moral character than the encouragement of business entrepreneurs. The only real war against poverty, he said, was fought by capitalists. This entrepreneurial thesis had never been a traditional conservative position, but an industrial capitalist defense. Andrew Carnegie, the steel capitalist, had developed this case against shooting the millionaires in 1891. Only secular capitalists considered entrepreneurs, and not moral virtue, most important in abolishing poverty. To be sure, Gilder could say that "the only dependable route from poverty is always work, family and faith," but he tellingly omitted thrift from the requirements because his faith rested on the entrepreneurs rather than any old-fashioned Protestant ethic. Individual thrift simply was not as important to Gilder and Reagan as the millionaires who deserved support because they employed people.[11]

Rather than being conservative, Reagan's supply-side economics was the Keynesian John F. Kennedy tax cut. In the more savage language of Alfred L. Malabre, Jr., economics editor of the *Wall Street Journal*, supply-side economics was "hokum" and a "grotesque" illustration of American "national self-indulgence." This theory, advocated largely by non-economists, offered a wonderful platform on which to run for the presidency. In the words of Malabre, it promised "the proverbial free lunch, a perfectly painless—almost magical—way in which to strengthen the economy, cut the budget deficit, and take a large step toward economic utopia." Once in power, the supply-siders demonstrated their "ideological expression of our extravagance, our effort to keep on living beyond our means" by refusing to support budget balancing. Reagan's economic theorists—Jack Kemp, Jude Wanniski, Paul Craig Roberts, Irving Kristol, and Arthur Laffer—were spenders who refused to support budget balancing. Despite much pretense of budget cutting, the Reagan administration created more deficit spending than all Democratic presidents combined. In *Beyond Our Means*, Malabre wrote that Reagan spent us "beyond our means to put things right."[12]

Republicans as well as Democrats had been hooked on debt. For a generation, Congress had been running a modest $26 billion annual budget shortage. The long tradition of Democratic

Congresses had demonstrated the excellent politics of voting benefits for constituents. Even Republicans learned to enjoy the popularity of spending. As former Republican Secretary of Commerce Peter G. Peterson (the son of frugal Greek immigrants) observed, the politics of debt had become a bipartisan addiction: "Congress and the Administration invent countless reasons why solving the problem can be postponed just a bit longer or why the deficit can't really be doing us that much harm."[13]

Congress preferred to let others solve national economic troubles. Consider the handling of high inflation, which had become politically intolerable by the end of the seventies. Politicians found their solution in the advice of Milton Friedman, whose monetarism actually required no cuts in government spending, no higher taxes. Friedman had revived the old quantity theory of money—that prices rise or fall as the supply of money grows or shrinks. The new miracle for politicians required restraint only by the Federal Reserve System. According to their indefatigable advocate of monetarism, if the Fed inhibited money creation by raising interest rates, stable prices were inevitable. The Friedman policy, enacted by Fed chairman Paul Volcker in 1979, brought inflation down with the severe economic slump of 1982. But high interest rates also brought a rising dollar and a disastrous trade deficit: Our goods became too expensive to sell, and cheaper foreign products flooded our market. American industrial manufacturing dwindled, workers went unemployed, and the $17 billion trade surplus of 1980 collapsed to a $139 billion deficit in 1986. The negative effects of this trade deficit and unemployment were, of course, offset and papered over by expansive national borrowing.[14] To use the metaphor of Senator Daniel Moynihan, the 1980s were a time when the United States "borrowed a trillion dollars from the Japanese and threw a party." The language of financier and immigrant Felix Rohatyn is more severe: "In an act of the ultimate financial cowardice, we have attempted to pass on to our children the cost of this behavior by borrowing from tomorrow instead of taxing today."[15]

As the twin national troubles—budget and trade deficits—ballooned, so did personal debt. When journalists pointed with alarm the rock-bottom low savings rate of 1.9 percent in the fall of 1985, a rosy business press quickly reassured Americans that they were not spendthrifts; there was no need for self-flagellation. The media was wrong, *Forbes* said, to think savings consisted only of money not spent. For more than a generation, Keynesians had also counted money spent for durable goods as savings. Even the government counted home purchases as investments, and that brought the personal savings rate for the third quarter of 1985 up to 3.4 percent. When padded with the savings of corporations, the national savings rate looked even better. Besides, *Forbes* insisted, more savings would only cause trouble for the economy. Economists from Harvard and Penn were quoted as supporting continued consumption. "It's not as though the more saving you do, the better off the economy is," they said. And: "There's no reason to save for savings sake and defer consumption." In short, "Only a miser saves for the sake of saving."[16]

While the popular Keynesian wisdom of consumption persisted, Keynesianism had lapsed into disrepute among academics for its failure to explain inflation. Academic economists had grown concerned about the American future, and Lester C. Thurow of MIT penned two popular criticisms of consumption, *Dangerous Currents: The State of Economics* (1983) and *Zero Sum Solution: Building a World Class Economy* (1985). By living beyond current means, Americans were penalizing their children and grandchildren, who would be forced to pay a larger and larger percentage of the gross national product to the thrifty foreigners who had financed our national debt. With the lowest savings rate in the industrial world—only one-third of Japan's—we could never save enough to invest in the tools, plant, and equipment necessary to keep American workers competitive in the world market. Thurow had no faith in sermonizing. To reduce spending, he recommended government restrictions on consumer credit and higher sales taxes on consumption buying.[17]

Such controls on consumption represented a return to the traditional conservative thrift that Reagan advisers opposed. Reagan's free-market theorists argued that government must stay out of the auction and leave individuals to act without government influence. This modern, secular theory ignores the American tradition of social forces—church, school, and government preaching of savings and self-restraint. Moral neutrality is a twentieth-century invention wherein all concepts of right and wrong are equally valid. It was this contemporary cultural relativism that Allan Bloom denounced in *The Closing of the American Mind* (1987). American history and culture were never really value-neutral; institutions have merely shifted from saving to spending as the right policy for promoting the general good.

Neither are other nations morally neutral. Take Japan, for example. As a peasant people, the Japanese shared the tradition of hard work and frugality required for survival by all agricultural peoples. This peasant tradition—in which wealth is accumulated only after generations of toil—was supported by Confucian, Shinto, and Buddhist traditions that made virtues of industry, honesty, and thrift. The wisdom of the ancients blended together into the early-nineteenth-century Hotoku movement, which placed the individual as a link in the generations of families and insisted that the wealth of each depended on parents and ancestors. The individual link must faithfully accumulate for descendants, the village, and the world. What the Protestant ethic taught Americans, the Hotoku tradition instructed Japanese: "Work much, earn much, and spend little. Gather plenty of fuel, but burn as little as possible. This is the secret of making a country wealthy; it is not miserliness. . . . We must save and provide for the future by industrious effort, the earnings of this year providing for the necessities of next year. Savings is the virtue of self-denial."[18]

When the feudal, agricultural society in Japan ended (little more than a century ago), the rural population provided an obedient, hard-working, and frugal labor force. The Japanese ethic was favorable to industrial development, and the nation quickly modernized without losing the traditional ethic. After the destruction of Japanese power by America in World War II, patriotism reinforced traditional Japanese asceticism as a means of rebuilding the country. The Japanese have remained low consumers and high savers with the encouragement of a government policy against easy credit. The tools of econometrics cannot prove that Japan's frugality ethic has produced the steady increase in its personal savings rate since the 1950s, but who can doubt that high savings and investment reflect Japan's cultural nationalism? Moral education, with its emphasis on self-restraint and concern for the community, has worked against consumption in Japan—just as advertising, government, economic education, and a culture of narcissism since the 1920s have promoted spending and debt in the United States.[19]

To be sure, some Americans resist the consumption ethic. Christian bookstores sell biblical guides—*Master Your Money* (1986), *Your Finances in Changing Times* (1982), and *Using Your Money Wisely* (1985)—that would tear up all credit cards and prohibit lavish consumption. "He who loves pleasure will become a poor man" (Proverbs 21:17), and "Keep out of debt and owe no man anything, except to love one another" (Romans 13:8) are favorite quotes. However, although a few books continue the traditional ascetic Christianity, more shelf space is devoted to a permissive culture, with extensive selections in psychology, cooking, and sex. Typical Christian literature now includes much applause of leisure, but little or none for thrift and savings. Not only are Christian bookstores reflections of the consumption ethic, but so are television evangelists. Take, for example, Jim and Tammy Bakker soliciting the spending of recreation dollars at their Heritage USA theme park. Although some poor congregations might still have ministers who preach traditional Christian self-denial, no white or black John Wesleys have appeared to do for the underclass in American ghettos what the Methodists did for the working class in eighteenth-century Britain.[20]

Among the dwindling farm population, those attempting to save the family farm speak of debt and spending with old-fashioned indignation. Even Americans who grew up in small towns around farmers, or with parents who were from farms, frequently manifest traditional peasant disdain for the consumption society. But rural traditionalists are few and growing fewer.

The revival of school banking might be considered a hopeful sign of turning values. After the inflation of the late sixties and early seventies proved so disastrous to savings banks and their depositors, school banking faded away. The revival began after Massachusetts bank examiners busted a sixth-grade bank in April 1983, threatening the Easton Middle School children with a $10,000 fine and ten years in state prison. Public outrage with the bank examiners stimulated a renaissance of school banking. But, upon closer examination, savings was never the issue in Massachusetts. The Easton Co-operative Bank had been a lending and not a savings bank. Children who forgot their 25 cents for milk or 75 cents for lunch could borrow the needed funds for penny-a-day interest. State bank examiners calculated that these pennies could add up to more than 365 percent—a usurious rate higher than the state's 23 percent bank lending maximum. The sixth graders visited the state legislature and won an exemption for their small bank. Other educational banks were organized in the wake of the Easton media event, with the greatest attention focused on the 20 high school banks that offered vocational training for students who ran full-service branch banks in the schools. In addition to accepting deposits, students operated computer terminals, loaned money, and sold travelers checks. The new Massachusetts programs were established to teach banking, not thrift, and the same purpose dominated on the national level, with the American Bankers Association organizing a Personal Economics Program (PEP) to teach young people about banking. Credit received more attention than savings in the PEP program, which included savings as but one part of "personal money management." These banks were selling banking, not reviving the old language of thrift and virtue.[21]

Among new immigrants, thrift continues to be striking in the Asians. Consider the Koreans, who have moved into small business across urban America, replacing Jews and Italians. In New York City, they have taken over the green grocery business. One young Korean, Jay Kwon arrived in 1972 with 75 dollars, and within a decade, worked his way up from janitor to factory labor foreman, saved $20,000, and bought a Brooklyn store. There he worked 12-hour days—cleaning, displaying, and selling produce—and endured many robberies. The modest profits he saved will put the next generation into a better retail enterprise. Savings and family capitalism still flourish in urban America.[22]

Cuban immigrants have restored a decaying Miami to prosperity and made Florida the center of Latin American trade. In their relatively few years in America, Spanish-Americans have generally moved ahead of blacks in asset ownership. Spanish families also save more than black families, who have most fully absorbed the American consumer ethic. The average black family in 1984 had assets of $3,400, whereas Spanish families held $4,910 and white families $39,140. This difference in assets was more than a difference in income. Comparing white and black families in the same income group, whites saved two to twelve times more than blacks. And these white Americans, after all, saved only one-third as much as the Japanese, the Greeks, or the Swiss.[23]

America long ago ceased to have a culture of thrift. To be sure, for a century following the American Revolution, major institutions preached self-restraint—making thrift part of the public creed and maintaining an average personal savings rate for urban people of about 15 percent. But the reputation of the virtue declined as thrift became associated with unwelcome immigrants. Once public faith in saving money ended—and church, school, and state ceased to recommend frugality—the American personal savings rate dropped to the lowest in the industrial world.[24]

Politicians were even more profligate than the citizens who elected them. Individuals saved at least something, but federal politicians spent until their deficits reduced national savings (government and private savings combined) to almost zero. Politicians put America into hock, increasing military spending while cutting taxes, to maintain the American empire. English-educated Paul Kennedy concluded in *The Rise and Fall of Great Powers* (1987) that America was in decline, a victim of the age-old curse of empires—overextending military commitments that citizens and their economies would no longer sustain.

The consumption society permitted its national government to continue enlarging the mountain of federal deficits. Although voters endorsed the general idea of balanced budgets, in practice they refused higher taxes and reduced spending—the means for bringing the budget into balance. A full 60 percent of voters were not worried enough about deficits to support either higher taxes or spending cuts. Congress was therefore unable to move towards a balanced budget until Phil Gramm blackmailed the leadership into accepting his Gramm-Rudman-Hollings deficit reduction amendment. Hollings refused to permit Congress to raise the debt ceiling to $2 trillion in 1985 unless it first allowed his deficit-reduction amendment to be adopted. The Texas-economist-turned-conservative-Republican-Senator   legislated an across-the-board cut of $11.7 billion in 1986, to be followed by automatic $36 billion annual slashes of the deficit.[25]

But Congress did not want to balance the budget. Even the Black Monday stock market crash of October 19, 1987 failed to put congressional leaders in a budget-cutting mood. A month of hard bargaining following the crash produced only an alternative cosmetic agreement, "a miserable little pittance" of $11.6 billion in cuts, a possible $9 billion in new taxes, and some accounting deceptions to evade the deeper 1987 Gramm-Rudman cuts. Congress and the President refused to even touch the estimated $10 trillion in unfunded future liabilities for Social Security, Medicare, and federal pensions. If these entitlement benefits were not reduced, according to Peter G. Peterson, budget-cutting efforts would never succeed. Even though more than 175 top corporate executives joined Peterson in a two-page advertisement in the *New York Times* and *Washington Post* demanding that Congress "rescue our economy" by cutting everything except "programs for the poor," politicians laughed at the appeal. "Listening to these representatives of corporate America talk about deficit reduction is like listening to the Reverend Jim Bakker preach the glory of chastity," quipped California Representative Fordney Stark. "At the same time they're preaching sacrifice they're in here looking for special favors." Congress and the public simply did not take budget balancing seriously.[26]

The American government reflected the debt culture of its people. Doubling the national debt did not trouble the Reagan administration, even though it also meant doubling the payment of interest: Interest on the 1988 public debt was estimated at $210 billion, or 20 percent of the trillion-dollar budget. Debt costs were, to be sure, usually understated by subtracting federal trust fund earnings and reporting "net interest" at only 14 percent of the budget. President Reagan made no apology for adding $1.5 trillion to the national debt. His *Economic Report 1988* repeated the rosy predictions of continued economic expansion and ever-rising standards of living. He worried only that Congress might increase taxes or legislate protection of manufacturing. Rather than calling for moral restraint on spending, Reagan repeated rhetorical calls for a constitutional amendment to force the federal government to live within a balanced budget. Debt held no real terror for Reagan; economic growth financed by his Treasury credit card was nothing to worry about. Although his economic advisers might concede that the low rate of national saving (3.2 percent for the 1980s) could pose a problem for future growth, they reassured Americans that a new definition of savings would make them feel better. Why not redefine savings to include money spent for research and human capital? That is, why not consider money spent for education, books, psychoanalysis, health care, and Aid to Families with Dependent Children as savings. With this creative solution—declaring spending to be saving—Reagan economists reassured Americans that they need not worry even though, by the old definition, their savings was the lowest in the industrial world.[27]

Reagan completed his presidency with great applause. Journalists wrote of "The Magic of Reaganomics," and the president's economics tutor, Milton Friedman, actually defended his twin deficits as "beneficial." We weren't Brazil or Mexico, for whom debt was a disaster, Friedman explained; America had not lived beyond its national income. Scare talk of deficits was only Democratic deceit, "rattling the scarecrow of deficits to frighten the public . . . into accepting higher taxes." The real problems, Friedman explained, were "excessive and wasteful government spending and taxing. . . . Congress will spend whatever the tax system yields plus the highest deficit the public will accept." By boldly running up the deficit, Friedman said, Reagan had put a restraint on congressional spending. Indeed, magic is the only accurate way to describe the Friedman-Reagan logic—that deficits would eventually produce savings, and consumer spending would create foreign investment that would result in economic growth similar to that of nineteenth-century America. The economist and his President did not speak from the traditional culture of frugality and thrift. The language of the White House had transcended that of Adam Smith and even John Maynard Keynes to voice a magical performance, part Milton Friedman and part Hollywood.[28]

Americans and their government continue to live beyond their means. Little hope exists for restoring a practice that has always been difficult and unpopular. Politicians will not legislate stiff consumption taxes as long as voters refuse to believe in personal saving. To be sure, budget director Richard G. Darman can join thrifty immigrants in lecturing Americans for acting as spoiled children—for practicing "cultural now-now-ism" for "self-indulgent theft from the future"—but all preaching of financial retrenchment will be ineffectual as long as credit continues to feed personal and public desires. A majority of economists may believe that America should reduce her $3 trillion debt, but the media gives almost equal time to those who ridicule any concern about the deficit.[29]

Americans will surely continue to ignore the wisdom of history—that thrift is essential for survival—until actual economic catastrophe strikes. Then the history of thrift will become a treasured memory as we struggle to survive with a sharply reduced standard of living. We will then celebrate the thrift of ancestors and immigrants who helped to build the American century of prosperity that endured only briefly after the restraint of elders no longer transmitted to children who abandoned the very concept of virtue that had built the inheritance.

Notes

CHAPTER 1

1. Hesiod, "Works and Days," in *The Homeric Hymns and Homerica*, translated by Hugh G. Evelyn-White (London: William Heinemann, 1914), 27, 33.

2. For an excellent review of peasant literature, see George M. Foster, "Peasant Society and the Image of Limited Good," *American Anthropologist* 67 (April 1965), 293–315.

3. Hsiao-Tung Fei and Chih-I Chang, *Earthbound in China: A Study of Rural Economy in Yunnan* (Chicago: University of Chicago Press, 1945), 82, 84, 119–120, 277.

4. Ibid., 265; Foster, "Peasant Society and the Image of Limited Good," 305.

5. Cato, *On Farming*, translated by Ernest Brehaut (New York: Columbia University Press, 1933), 8; M. I. Finley, *The Ancient Economy* (Berkeley: University of California Press, 1973), 58; Alan E. Astin, *Cato the Censor* (Oxford: Clarendon Press, 1978), 1–3, 83, 94, 293.

6. Radoslav A. Tsanoff, *The Moral Ideals of Our Civilization* (New York: E. P. Dutton, 1942), 36, 46–47, 55, 57.

7. Jacques Le Goff, *Medieval Civilization 400–1500* (New York: Basil Blackwell, 1989), 222–225, 317–318.

8. H. H. Ben-Sasson, *A History of the Jewish People* (Cambridge: Harvard University Press, 1976), 390–394, 471, 639.

9. Fernand Braudel, *The Wheels of Commerce*, vol. II of *Civilization and Capitalism* (New York: Harper & Row, 1982), 559–563; Lester K. Little, "Pride Goes before Avarice: Social Change and the Vices in Latin Christendom," *American Historican Review* 76 (February 1971), 16–49.

10. Braudel, *The Wheels of Commerce*, 578–581.

11. Michel Mollat, *The Poor in the Middle Ages: An Essay in Social History*, translated by Arthur Goldhammer (New Haven: Yale University Press, 1986), 254–260, 290–291.

12. Roland H. Bainton, *Here I Stand: A Life of Martin Luther* (Nashville: Abingdon Press, 1950), 236–238; Theodore G. Tappert, ed., *Selected Writings of Martin Luther 1517–1520*, vol. 1 (Philadelphia: Fortress Press, 1967), 188–190, 318–319, 350.

13. Braudel, *The Wheels of Commerce*, 570; W. G. Hoskins, *The Midland Peasant* (London: Macmillan, 1957), 53, 142; Alan Macfarlane, *The Origins of English Individualism* (Oxford: Basil Blackwell, 1978), 76–78, 196–197.

14. Dorothy Hartley, ed., *Thomas Tusser: His Good Points of Husbandry* (New York: Augustus M. Kelly, 1970), 158–159.

15. Henry Peacham, *The Worth of a Peny or a Caution to keep Money* (London: S. Griffen, 1664), 15, 7, 17, 25, 34.

16. Thomas Mun, *England's Treasure by Forraign Trade* (Oxford: Basil Blackwell, 1949), 72–73.

17. George Mackenzie, *The Moral History of Frugality* (London, 1691), 2–3, 92.

18. Leonard W. Labaree, ed., *The Papers of Benjamin Franklin*, vol. 7 (New Haven: Yale University Press, 1963), 342–349.

19. *The Autobiography of Benjamin Franklin*, edited by Leonard W. Labaree et al. (New Haven: Yale University Press, 1964), 148–150. For the secularism of Franklin, see J. E. Crowley, *This Sheba, Self: The Conceptualization of Economic Life in Eighteenth-Century America* (Baltimore: Johns Hopkins University Press, 1979), 122–123.

20. Labaree, *The Papers of Benjamin Franklin*, vol. 3, 475.

21. Adam Smith, *An Inquiry into the Nature and Causes of the Wealth of Nations*, edited by Edwin Cannan (Chicago: University of Chicago Press, 1976), 362–363; R. J. Holton, *The Transition from Feudalism to Capitalism* (New York: St. Martins Press, 1985), 36–37; Albert O. Hirschman, *The Passions and the Interests: Political Arguments for Capitalism before its Triumph* (Princeton: Princeton University Press, 1977), 60, 71, 110–111.

22. Smith, *Wealth of Nations*, 359.

23. Edmund S. Morgan, "The Puritan Ethic and the American Revolution," *William and Mary Quarterly* 24 (January 1967), 3–15.

24. T. H. Breen, *Tobacco Culture: The Mentality of the Great Tidewater Planters on the Eve of Revolution* (Princeton: Princeton University Press, 1985), 36–37, 130, 191–193, 230.

25. Garry Wills, *Cincinnatus: George Washington and the Enlightenment* (Garden City: Doubleday, 1984), 133–137, 217; Meyer Reinhold, *The Classick Pages* (University Park: Pennsylvania State University, 1975), 147–150; Frederic M. Litto, "Addison's *Cato* in the Colonies," *William and Mary Quarterly* 23 (July 1966), 430–449.

26. Forrest McDonald, *Novus Ordo Seclorum: The Intellectual Origins of the Constitution* (Lawrence: University Press of Kansas, 1985), 68–75, 88–90; David E. Shi, *The Simple Life: Plain Living and High Thinking in American Culture* (New York: Oxford University Press, 1985), 56–75.

CHAPTER 2

1. Alexis de Tocqueville, *Democracy in America*, edited by J. P. Mayer (New York: Harper & Row, 1966), 615, 291–292, 444, 284–285, 529.

2. From the large literature dealing with the Weber thesis, one might read R. H. Tawney, *Religion and the Rise of Capitalism* (London: John Murray, 1926), 226–227, 319–321; Kurt Samuelsson, *Religion and Economic Action*, translated by E. Geoffrey French (New York: Basic Books, 1961), 28–34, 151–152; R. J. Holton, *The Transition from Feudalism to Capitalism* (New York: St. Martins Press, 1985), 109–125; and Gordon Marshall, *In Search of the Spirit of Capitalism* (London: Hutchinson, 1982). See also "Symposium on Weber's The Protestant Ethic," *Telos* (Winter 1988–89), 71–108.

3. Max Weber, *The Protestant Ethic and the Spirit of Capitalism*, translated by Talcott Parsons (New York: Scribner's, 1958), 97–115; James A. Henretta, *The Evolution of American Society 1700–1815* (Lexington, MA: D. C. Heath, 1973), 98–102; Marshall, *In Search of the Spirit of Capitalism*, 72–75.

4. Stephen Foster, *Their Solitary Way: The Puritan Social Ethic in the First Century of Settlement in New England* (New Haven: Yale University Press, 1971), 109–110.

5. Ibid., 104.

6. Ibid., 107–108.

7. Ibid., 109, 116–118, 125–126; Sacvan Bercovitch, *The American Jeremiad* (Madison: University of Wisconsin Press, 1978).

8. Richard L. Bushman, *From Puritan to Yankee: Character and the Social Order in Connecticut 1690–1765* (Cambridge: Harvard University Press, 1967), 188; J. E. Crowley, *This Sheba, Self: The Conceptualization of Economic Life in Eighteenth-Century America* (Baltimore: Johns Hopkins University Press, 1974), 76–78.

9. Philip Greven, *The Protestant Temperament: Patterns of Child-Rear-*

ing, Religious Experience, and the Self in Early America (New York: Alfred A. Knopf, 1977), 13–50.

10. E. P. Thompson, *The Making of the English Working Class* (New York: Pantheon Books, 1964), 37–38, 357–379; Marshall, *In Search of the Spirit of Capitalism*, 77–79; Weber, *The Protestant Ethic*, 175.

11. E. P. Thompson, "Time, Work-Discipline, and Industrial Capitalism," *Past and Present* 38 (December 1967), 88–91.

12. Bernard Semmel, *The Methodist Revolution* (New York: Basic Books, 1973), 3–8, 72–73.

13. John Wesley, *The Works of John Wesley*, vol. 6 (Grand Rapids: Zondervan Publishing House, 1958), 130–133.

14. Quoted from Weber, *The Protestant Ethic*, 175.

15. To find frugal and industrious advice, see *Methodist Magazine*, vol. 2 (1819), 392, and vol. 4 (1821), 474.

16. Charles G. Steffen, *The Mechanics of Baltimore: Workers and Politics in the Age of Revolution 1763–1812* (Urbana: University of Illinois Press, 1984), 253–263.

17. Paul Faler, "Cultural Aspects of the Industrial Revolution: Lynn, Massachusetts, Shoemakers and Industrial Morality, 1826–1860," *Labor History* 15 (Summer 1974), 367–394; Faler, *Mechanic and Manufacturers in the Early Industrial Revolution: Lynn, Massachusetts 1780–1860* (Albany: State University of New York Press, 1981), 45–47, 102–103.

18. Bruce Laurie, "Nothing on Compulsion: Life Styles of Philadelphia Artisans, 1820–1850," *Labor History* 15 (Summer 1974), 337–366; Laurie, *Working People of Philadelphia 1800–1850* (Philadelphia: Temple University Press, 1980), 42–44, 48–51, 56–57, 117–119, 142–143.

19. Greven, *The Protestant Temperament*, 269–313; Thomas M. Doerflinger, in *A Vigorous Spirit of Enterprise: Merchants & Economic Development in Revolutionary Philadelphia* (Chapel Hill: University of North Carolina Press, 1986), 161–164, found both ascetic and indulgent capitalists in Philadelphia. The materialistic evidence that riches tended to remain in merchant families despite their lack of virtue is developed by Edward Pessen, *Riches, Class and Power Before the Civil War* (Lexington, MA: D. C. Heath, 1973), 84–89, 137, 140, 148, 151.

20. Tocqueville, *Democracy in America*, 533.

21. Capitalist control of the bourgeois culture is argued by Paul Faler, Alan Dawley, and Paul E. Johnson. Bruce Laurie argues that evangelical workers voluntarily chose their own culture of self-restraint and profited from it.

CHAPTER 3

1. Traditional biographies are Ruth E. Finley's *The Lady of Godey's: Sarah Josepha Hale* (Philadelphia: J. B. Lippincott, 1931) and Isabelle

Webb Entrinkin's *Sarah Josepha Hale and Godey's Lady's Book* (Philadelphia: Lancaster Press, 1946). For a feminist view, see Ann Douglas, *The Feminization of American Culture* (New York: Alfred A. Knopf, 1977), 6, 45, 78–79. A recent biography is Sherbrooke Rogers, *Sarah Josepha Hale: A New England Pioneer* (Grantham, NH: Thompson and Ruther, 1985).

2. Sarah J. Hale, *Sketches of American Character* (Boston: Putnam & Hunt, 1829), 287; Rogers, *Sarah Josepha Hale*, 11–22; Finley, *The Lady of Godey's*, 27–36.

3. See Hale's obituary of Sedgwick in *Godey's Lady's Book*, November, 1867, 448, and Edward Halsey Foster, *Catherine Maria Sedgwick* (New York: Twayne Publishers, 1974).

4. *Northwood* has been interpreted as sectional literature by William R. Taylor, *Cavalier and Yankee: The Old South and American National Character* (New York: George Braziller, 1961), 115–135.

5. Sarah J. Hale, "Fifty Years of My Literary Life," *Godey's Lady's Book*, December 1877, 522.

6. Ibid., "The Conversazione," January 1837, 5.

7. Ibid., "Editor's Table," April 1863, 396; June 1863, 577–578. The translation is from the 1976 *Good News* Bible.

8. Sarah J. Hale, "The Influence of Fashions," Boston *Ladies Magazine*, January, 1832, 1–3; August 1829, 372–378.

9. Ibid., *Traits of American Life* (Philadelphia: Carey & Hart, 1835), 372–373.

10. Ibid., "The Times," Boston *Ladies Magazine*, August, 1829, 372–378.

11. Ibid., "The Worth of Money," February 1830, 49–55.

12. Ibid., "Letter on Cholera," July 1832, 318–325; "How Shall We Help the Poor?" *Godey's Lady's Book*, February 1867, 190–191.

13. Rogers, *Sarah Josepha Hale*, 53–64.

14. Sarah J. Hale, Critical review of Child's *The Frugal Housewife* in Boston *Ladies Magazine*, January, 1830, 42–43.

15. Ibid., "Domestic Economy," *Godey's Lady's Book*, January 1840, 43.

16. Ibid., "Editor's Table," June 1837, 285; "Women of America," Boston *Ladies Magazine*, May 1830, 205–206.

17. Ibid., "Editor's Table," *Godey's Lady's Book*, July 1844, 45.

18. Ibid., *Keeping House and House Keeping: A Story of Domestic Life* (New York: Harper & Brothers, 1845), 20–22, 95–97.

19. Ibid., 107–108.

20. Ibid., 139–140.

21. For the plain tradition, see David E. Shi, *The Simple Life: Plain Living and High Thinking in American Culture* (New York: Oxford University Press, 1985), 50–91.

22. Sarah J. Hale, "Editor's Table," *Godey's Lady's Book*, June 1843, 293; December 1852, 576; February 1856, 177.

23. Ibid., December 1850, 380; May 1852, 404–405; January 1855, 75.

24. Ibid., February 1841, 95.

25. Ibid., July 1850, 58.

26. Ibid., March 1866, 278.

27. Ibid., January 1876, 90–91; November 1876, 473. Moralistic males also preached repentance from style, extravagance, and dissipation during the hard times of every business cycle. See Murray N. Rothbard, *The Panic of 1819: Reactions and Policies* (New York: Columbia University Press, 1962), 20–23; Samuel Rezneck, "The Influence of Depression upon American Opinion, 1857–1859," *Journal of Economic History* II (May 1942), 6–7; Eric Foner, *Free Soil, Free Labor, Free Men: The Ideology of the Republican Party Before the Civil War* (New York: Oxford University Press, 1970), 24–27.

28. For the traditional women's culture, see Anne L. Kuhn, *The Mother's Role in Childhood Education: New England Concepts 1830–1860* (New Haven: Yale University Press, 1947); Mary P. Ryan, *The Empire of Mother: American Writing about Domesticity* (New York: Haworth Press, 1982); and Nancy F. Cott, *The Bonds of Womanhood: "Woman's Sphere" in New England, 1780–1835* (New Haven: Yale University Press, 1977).

CHAPTER 4

1. Willard Phillips, *A Manual of Political Economy* (Boston: Hilliard, Gray, 1828), 158.

2. Gertrude Himmelfarb, *The Idea of Poverty: England in the Early Industrial Age* (New York: Alfred A. Knopf, 1984), 12, 100–143.

3. Reverend Duncan's savings bank was certainly not the first; even he admitted the existence of an earlier one. See Henry Duncan, *An Essay on the Nature and Advantages of Parish Banks* (1816), 36–37.

4. "Parish or Savings Banks," *Edinburgh Review* 25 (June 1815), 135–146.

5. William Davis, *Friendly Advice to Industrious and Frugal Persons Recommending Provident Institutions or Savings Banks* (London: Bensley & Son, 1817), 7–18.

6. Quoted from Emerson Keyes, *A History of Savings Banks in the United States 1816–1874* (New York: Bradford Rhodes, 1876), 38–39.

7. New York Society for the Prevention of Pauperism, *Documents* (1818), 7; reprinted in Fritz Redlich, *The Molding of American Banking*, vol. 2 (New York: Hafner Publishing Co., 1951) 214–215, and in Weldon Welfling, *Mutual Savings Banks: The Evolution of a Financial Intermediary*

(Cleveland: Case Western Reserve University, 1968), 21–22. Redlich denies that a majority of savings bank founders were philanthropists. He thinks them self-interested businessmen and politicians. See his *Molding of American Banking*, 216. Philanthropists clearly dominated the savings bank movement, and Redlich is not correct in saying that Christians weren't even conspicuous among Philadelphia founders. Condy Raguet, the Philadelphia leader, attributed his public conduct to his Swedenborg faith. See: "Sketch of the Life and Character of Condy Raguet," *Hunt's Merchant Magazine* 7 (December 1842), 542–543.

8. Keyes, *Savings Banks in the United States*, 309.

9. Ibid., 319. A discussion of the report can also be found in Raymond A. Mohl, *Poverty in New York 1783–1825* (New York: Oxford University Press, 1971), 246.

10. Welfling, *Mutual Savings Banks*, 22.

11. For a critical discussion of "social control" theories, see Lois W. Banner, "Religious Benevolence as Social Control: A Critique of an Interpretation," *Journal of American History* 60 (June 1973), 23–41. Keyes, *Savings Banks in the United States*, I, 201, quotes a Portsmouth, New Hampshire contemporary as saying: "The bank organized here soon after the Sunday school was established, and for the same purpose, and to a considerable extent, by the same persons. It was essentially a philanthropic enterprise, intended to elevate the character and improve the condition of young people and people of small means."

12. Willard Phillips, *A Manual of Political Economy* (Boston: Hilliard, Gray, 1828), 74–75, 158.

13. Thomas Cooper, *Lectures on the Elements of Political Economy*, 2nd ed. (Columbia: McMorris & Wilson, 1827), 7, 302, 308–309.

14. Francis Wayland, *The Elements of Moral Science*, edited by Joseph L. Blau (Cambridge: Harvard University Press, 1963), 340–353.

15. Daniel Raymond, *The Elements of Political Economy* (Baltimore: F. Lucas Jr., 1823), 413.

16. For urban problems, see Charles E. Rosenberg, *The Cholera Years* (Chicago: University of Chicago Press, 1962), 44; James C. Wharton, *Crusaders for Fitness: The History of American Health Reformers* (Princeton: Princeton University Press, 1982), 38–45; and Stephen Nissenbaum, *Sex, Diet and Debility in Jacksonian America: Sylvester Graham and Health Reform* (Westport, CT: Greenwood Press, 1980), 4–8. For hostility to cities, see Richard Hofstadter, *The Age of Reform* (New York: Knopf, 1955) 23–34; and Morton and Lucia White, *The Intellectual versus the City: From Thomas Jefferson to Frank Lloyd Wright* (Cambridge: Harvard University Press, 1962), 21–53.

17. Carl David Arfwedson, *The United States and Canada in 1832* vol. I (New York: Johnson Reprints, 1969), 120–124.

18. *The Jacksonians on the Poor* (New York: Arno Press, 1971), 9, 21, 41, 74–75, 81.

19. Reprinted in Freeman Hunt, *Worth and Wealth* (New York: Stringer & Townsend, 1856), 267–276.

20. Stephan Thernstrom, *Poverty and Progress: Social Mobility in a Nineteenth Century City* (Cambridge: Harvard University Press, 1964), 122–131. For a savings bank scoffer, see Paul G. Faler, *Mechanics and Manufacturers in the Early Industrial Revolution: Lynn, Massachusetts 1780–1860* (Albany: State University of New York Press, 1981), 161–163.

21. John Lintner, *Mutual Savings Banks in the Savings and Mortgage Markets* (Boston: Harvard Graduate School of Business Administration, 1948), 51–53, 473; John P. Townsend, "Savings Banks," *Journal of Social Science* 9 (January 1878), 47–61.

22. Alan Teck, *Mutual Saving Banks and Savings and Loan Associations* (New York: Columbia University Press, 1968), 19–32; Lintner, *Mutual Savings Banks*, 473.

23. Lintner, *Mutual Savings Banks*, 463; Morton Keller, *The Life Insurance Enterprise 1885–1910* (Cambridge: Harvard University Press, 1963), 10–11; Margaret F. Byington, *Homestead: The Households of a Mill Town* (New York: Charities Publications Committee, 1910), 90–91. To compare with the British working class, see Paul Johnson, *Saving and Spending: The Working-Class Economy in Britain, 1870–1939* (Oxford: Oxford University Press, 1985).

24. William Graham Sumner, ed., *A History of Banking*, vol II (New York: Journal of Banking, 1896), 458, 464; David A. Wells, *Recent Economic Changes* (New York: D. Appelton, 1890), 342, 344.

25. Mugwumps were most interested in taking money out of politics, a sentiment which contributed to the Federal Reserve System, but they had always been thrift activists for postal as well as savings banks. For postal savings, see Senate Committee on Post-Offices, 60th Congress, 1st session 1908, Senate Report 525, 1–145; E. W. Kemmerer, "The United States Postal Savings Bank," *Political Science Quarterly* 26 (September 1911), 462–499; and Henry F. Pringle, *The Life and Times of William Howard Taft* (New York: Holt, Rinehart, 1939), 516–520.

26. Edward L. Robinson, *One Hundred Years of Savings Banking* (American Banking Association, 1917), 18–19; "A Century of Savings Banks," *World's Work* 33 (December 1916), 124–125. The 14.7 percent personal savings rate for non-agricultural individuals is from Raymond W. Goldsmith, *A Study of Savings in the United States* vol. I (Princeton: Princeton University Press, 1955), 241.

CHAPTER 5

1. Diane Ravitch, *The Great School Wars: New York City, 1805–1973* (New York: Basic Books, 1974), 3–26; Carl F. Kaestle, *The Evolution of an Urban School System* (Cambridge: Harvard University Press, 1973), 81–113.

2. Timothy L. Smith, "Protestant Schooling and American Nationality, 1800–1850," *Journal of American History* 53 (March 1967), 679–680, 695.

3. Harry R. Warfel, *Noah Webster: Schoolmaster to America* (New York: Macmillan Company, 1936), 62–63; Noah Webster, *An American Selection of Lessons in Reading and Speaking* (Hartford: Hudson & Goodwin, 1789), 25.

4. I have used the 1982 "original McGuffey" reprints by Mott Media, Inc. The dominant "middle-class" interpretation of the readers has been Richard D. Mosier's *Making the American Mind: Social and Moral Ideas in the McGuffey Readers* (New York: Russell & Russell, 1947), which John A. Westerhoff [*McGuffey and his Readers: Piety, Morality, and Education in Nineteenth-Century America* (Nashville: Abingdon, 1978), 26] has exposed as resting on post–1850 editions. The superficial nature of McGuffey commentary also includes sales of McGuffey Readers. The pronouncement by the president of the American Book Company that 122 million had sold by the 1920s is insufficient evidence for repeating the number. The earlier publisher, Henry H. Vale [*A History of the McGuffey Readers* (Cleveland: Burrows Brothers, 1911), 47, 58–61] offers no such number. But ever since Mark Sullivan's *Our Times* vol. 2 (New York: Charles Scribners' Sons, 1927), the publisher's hype has been reported as truth.

5. "Common Schools," *Princeton Review* 38 (January 1865), 38; "Romanism and our Common Schools," *Methodist Review* 52 (April 1870), 204–220.

6. Robert Michaelsen, *Piety in the Public Schools* (New York: Macmillan, 1970), 98; David D. Thompson, "Religious Instruction in the Public Schools," *Methodist Review* vol. 71 (January 1889), 96; "Instruction in Religion in our Schools," *Methodist Review* vol. 90 (November 1907), 899. The persistence of Protestantism can be found in David B. Tyack, "Onward Christian Soldiers: Religion in the American Common School," in *History and Education*, edited by Paul Nash (New York: Random House, 1970), 212–255.

7. Kurt F. Leidecker, *Yankee Teacher: The Life of William Torrey Harris* (New York: The Philosophical Library, 1946), 84. See also Merle Curti,

The Social Ideas of American Educators (New York: Charles Scribner's Sons, 1935), 310–347; Neil Gerard McCluskey, *Public Schools and Moral Education* (New York: Columbia University Press, 1958), 99–176; and Gerald Richard Lyons, "The Influence of Hegel on the Philosophy of Education of William Torrey Harris" (Ph.D. Dissertation, Boston University, 1964).

8. W. T. Harris, "Moral Education in Common Schools," *Journal of Social Science* 18 (May 1884), 122–134; "The President Need for Moral Training in the Public Schools," *Journal of Education* 27 (March 1, 1888), 131.

9. Harris as a mugwump can be found in Leidecker's *Yankee Teacher,* 460–461. For other views of mugwumps, see Geoffrey Blodgett, "The Mugwump Reputation, 1870 to the Present," *Journal of American History* 66 (March 1980), 867–887. The relevance of moral philosophy for mugwumps is stressed by James McLachlan in "American Colleges and the Transmission of Culture: The Case of the Mugwumps," in *The Hofstadter Aegis: A Memorial,* edited by Stanley Elkins and Eric McKitrick (New York: Knopf, 1974), 195–202.

10. Francis Wayland, *The Elements of Moral Science,* edited by Joseph L. Blau (Cambridge: Harvard University Press, 1963), xli–xlii, 327.

11. Daniel Walker Howe, *The Unitarian Conscience: Harvard Moral Philosophy 1805–1861* (Cambridge: Harvard University Press, 1970), 228; Hugh Hawkins, *Between Harvard and America: The Educational Leadership of Charles W. Eliot* (New York: Oxford University Press, 1972), 163, 149; F. W. Taussig, "Introduction" to *Economic Essays by Charles Franklin Dunbar,* edited by O. M. W. Sprague (New York: Macmillan Company, 1904), vii–ix.

12. "Economy Among the Middle Classes," *New York Times,* November 9, 1868; Charles F. Adams, Jr., "The Currency; Debate of 1873–74," *North American Review* 109 (July 1874), 142.

13. For mugwump outrage, see E. L. Godkin, "Commercial Immorality and Political Corruption," *North American Review* 107 (July 1868), 248–266; "The Tumble in Gold," *Harper's Weekly* 10 (March 24, 1866), 179; "Extravagance in Living," *New York Times,* October 19, 1877; and Francis Bowen, *American Political Economy* (New York, 1870), 342.

14. Henry Adams, "The New York Gold Conspiracy," *Westminister Review* (October 1870), reprinted in Charles Francis Adams, Jr. and Henry Adams, *Chapters of Erie* (Ithaca: Cornell University Press, 1956), 101–136, 135; Maury Klein, in *The Life and Legend of Jay Gould* (1986) contends that critics have exaggerated defects in the capitalist's character.

15. William Graham Sumner, *A History of American Currency* (New York: Henry Holt and Company, 1874), 248–250.

16. Charles F. Dunbar, "Economic Science in America, 1776–1876," *North American Review* 72 (January 1876), 144. Mugwump concern for economic issues in 1884 can be found in Horace White, "The Silver Crisis," *Nation* 38 (February 28, 1884), 182; J. Laurence Laughlin, "The Silver Danger," *Atlantic* 103 (May 1884), 681; Horace White, "Panics and Politics," *Nation* 39 (October 16, 1884), 325; and Edward Atkinson to William Fowler, October 29, 1884, (Atkinson Collection, Massachusetts Historical Society). For E. L. Godkin's view of Blaine as a speculator, see "The True Meaning of Blaine: The Presidency as a Business," *Nation* 39 (August 14, 1884), 126 and (October 16, 1884), 325.

17. For the Hegel influence, see Leidecker, *Yankee Teacher*, 316–324, and Lyons, "The Influence of Hegel on the Philosophy of Education of William Torrey Harris," 15–20; Harris, "The Church, the State, and the School," *North American Review* 133 (September 1881), 215–227; Harris, "Statistics versus Socialism," *Forum* 24 (October 1897), 186–199.

18. Leidecker, *Yankee Teacher*, 541. For an educator's fear that populists created a greater crisis than the revolution or the Civil War, see Nicholas Murray Butler, "Editorial," *Educational Review* 12 (November 1896), 404–406.

19. Bureau of Education, 51st Congress, 1st session, 1891, House Executive Document 2729, 655–668; Simon W. Straus, *History of the Thrift Movement in America* (Philadelphia: J. B. Lippincott, 1920), 35–36.

20. Sara Louisa Oberholtzer, "School Savings Banks," *Annals of the American Academy of Political and Social Science* 3 (July 1892), 15–28.

21. Bureau of Education, 656.

22. Ibid., 669.

23. Herbert H. Palmer, "Thrift in the High School," *Education* 35 (March 1915), 421–426; George Zook, "Thrift in the United States," *Annals of the American Academy of Political and Social Science* 87 (January 1920), 208.

24. Straus, *The Thrift Movement in America*, 62–73, 103, 119–121.

25. Simon W. Straus, "Thrift—an Educational Necessity," *National Education Association Proceedings* (1916), 196–201.

26. Kate Blake, "Thrift in Relation to the Home," *National Education Association Proceedings* (1916), 220–221.

CHAPTER 6

1. Eugene D. Genovese, *The Political Economy of Slavery* (New York: Vintage Books, 1967), 75; Genovese, *Roll, Jordan Roll: The World the Slaves Made* (New York: Random House, 1974), 311–312.

2. C. Vann Woodward, "The Southern Ethic in a Puritan World,"

168   Notes

William and Mary Quarterly 25 (July 1968), 343–370; Frederick Douglass, *Life and Times of Frederick Douglass* (New York: Collier Books, 1962), 60; Booker T. Washington, *Up From Slavery* (Boston: Houghton Mifflin, 1901), 33–34.

3. Grady McWhiney, *Cracker Culture: Celtic Ways in the Old South* (Tuscaloosa: University of Alabama Press, 1988), 43, 45, 253, 264.

4. Ira Berlin, *Slaves without Masters: The Free Negro in the Antebellum South* (New York: Oxford University Press, 1974), 244–249; William R. Hogan & Edwin A. Davis, eds., *William Johnson's Natchez: The Antebellum Diary of a Free Negro* (Baton Rouge: Louisiana State University Press, 1951); August Meier, *Negro Thought in America, 1880–1915* (Ann Arbor: University of Michigan Press, 1963), 5.

5. Jacqueline Jones, *Soldiers of Light and Love: Northern Teachers and Georgia Blacks 1865–1873* (Chapel Hill: University of North Carolina Press, 1980), 126; Robert C. Morris, *Reading, 'Riting, and Reconstruction* (Chicago: University of Chicago Press, 1981), 190–212; Joe M. Richardson, *Christian Reconstruction: The American Missionary Association and Southern Blacks, 1861–1890* (Athens: University of Georgia Press, 1986), 42–43.

6. Carl R. Osthaus, *Freedmen, Philanthropy, and Fraud: A History of the Freedman's Savings Bank* (Urbana: University of Illinois Press, 1976), 12–13.

7. U. S. Congress, *Freedmen's Bureau*, 39th Congress 1st session, 1866, House Executive Document 70, 347–349.

8. Walter L. Fleming, *The Freedmen's Savings Bank* (Chapel Hill: University of North Carolina Press, 1927), 145.

9. Ibid., 147.

10. Douglass, *Life and Times of Frederick Douglass*, 400–402.

11. Osthaus, *Freedmen, Philanthropy, and Fraud*, 138–140, 147, 151–173, 211–213, 221.

12. Emerson Keyes, *A History of Savings Banks in the United States 1816–1874*, vol. II (New York: Bradford Rhodes, 1878), 563–564; Osthaus, *Freedmen, Philanthropy, and Fraud*, 218–220.

13. James M. McPherson, *The Abolitionist Legacy: From Reconstruction to the NAACP* (Princeton: Princeton University Press, 1975), 71.

14. Roger L. Ransom & Richard Sutch, *One Kind of Freedom: The Economic Consequences of Emancipation* (Cambridge: Cambridge University Press, 1977), 4–6, 177; W.E.B. Du Bois, *The Souls of Black Folk* (New York: New American Library, 1969), 179–182.

15. E. Franklin Frazier, *Black Bourgeoisie: The Rise of a New Middle Class* (New York: Free Press, 1957), 60, 73–75; Louis R. Harlan, *Booker T. Washington: The Making of a Black Leader 1856–1901* (New York: Oxford University Press, 1972), 57–74.

16. Booker T. Washington, *Character Building* (New York: Doubleday, Page, 1902), 268–274.

17. David M. Tucker, *Arkansas: A People and Their Reputation* (Memphis: Memphis State University Press, 1985), 48–49.

18. Robert Higgs, "Accumulation of Property by Southern Blacks Before World War I," *American Economic Review* 72 (September 1982), 728–730, 735; Robert A. Margo, "Comment and Further Evidence," *American Economic Review* 74 (September 1984), 768–781.

19. Frazier, *Black Bourgeoisie*, 185–238.

20. For the old view, see Frederick L. Hoffman, *Race Traits and Tendencies of the American Negro* (New York: Macmillan, 1896), 306–307; Howard W. Odum, *Social and Mental Traits of the Negro* (New York: Columbia University Press, 1910), 224, 283; and Gunnar Myrdal, *An American Dilemma: The Negro Problem and Modern Democracy* (New York: Harper & Row, 1944), 367–369. The faulty statistics concerning black consumption are corrected by Marjorie Galenson in "Do Blacks Save More?" *The American Economic Review* 62 (March 1972), 211–215.

21. C. Eric Lincoln, *The Black Muslims in America* (Boston: Beacon Press, 1961), 91.

22. Thomas Sowell, *Ethnic America: A History* (New York: Basic Books, 1981), 282–283, 199, 219; Bureau of the Census, *Household Wealth and Asset Ownership: 1984* (Washington: Government Printing Office, 1986), 1–5.

CHAPTER 7

1. Arthur S. Link, ed., *The Papers of Woodrow Wilson*, vol. 42 (Princeton: Princeton University Press, 1983), 75. For thrift concern, see Daniel Horowitz, *The Morality of Spending: Attitudes toward the Consumer Society in America, 1875–1940* (Baltimore: Johns Hopkins University Press, 1985), 67–70; David E. Shi, *The Simple Life: Plain Living and High Thinking in American Culture* (New York: Oxford University Press, 1985), 215–216; Simon W. Straus, *History of the Thrift Movement in America* (Philadelphia: J. B. Lippincott, 1920), 68–70, 129–136; Donald McConnell, *Economic Virtues in the United States* (New York: Columbia University Press, 1930), 132–136.

2. *New York Times*, July 14, 1917; July 20, 1917; and August 19, 1917; Basil P. Blackett, "Address" (pamphlet), War Savings Division Records, Bureau of Public Debt, Record Group 53, National Archives. These 79 shelf-feet of records are only loosely organized because, according to Civil Archives Division head William F. Sherman, the past generation of researchers "almost never" showed any interest in them.

3. Pierre Jay to Secretary McAdoo, July 28, 1917; Report of Informal Conference, file 39, unnumbered box, War Savings Division.

4. *New York Times*, May 26, 1917; September 25, 1917; and September 26, 1917; George E. Roberts, "Frank Arthur Vanderlip," *Review of Reviews* 60 (July 1919), 50–60; Frank A. Vanderlip, *From Farm Boy to Financier* (New York: D. Appleton-Century, 1935), 221, 290–293; John J. Broesamle, *William Gibbs McAdoo: A Passion for Change 1863–1917* (Port Washington, NY: Kennikat, 1973), 148–149.

5. "Conference with Committee of Savings," October 12, 1917, 29, 267 (bound manuscript), War Savings Division Records.

6. *New York Times*, November 16, 1917; Frank A. Vanderlip, "How to Win the War," 11–13 (pamphlet), War Savings Division Records.

7. Dwight W. Morrow, "Speeches," 6, 13–21, 37–38 (booklet), War Savings Division Records; Morrow, "The Meaning of the War Savings Movement," *Academy of Political Science Proceedings* 7 (December 15, 1917), 711–714.

8. "National War Savings Committee Report," August 5, 1918 (bound volume), Conference Material 1917–20, Box 1, War Savings Division Records.

9. Thomas Nixon Carver, *War Thrift* (New York: Oxford University Press, 1919), 34, 52–59.

10. "Composite Questionnaire," August 17, 1918, 271–273, 453 (bound volume), War Savings Division Records.

11. "Minutes . . . of Campaign in Connecticut," December 5, 1917, 15, 29–30 (bound volume), War Savings Division Records; *New York Times*, December 9, 1917; December 30, 1917.

12. Nan Oppenlander-Eberle, *Good Fairy Thrift* (Swarthmore: Chatauqua Association of Pennsylvania, 1917), 9–10. (Copies in War Savings Division Records).

13. Harrison E. Salisbury, *A Journey For Our Times* (New York: Harper and Row, 1983), 10–11.

14. "Manual for Boy Scouts of America in War-Savings Stamps," *Scouting* 6 (1918), Box 5, War Savings Division Records.

15. "War Savings Societies," 1918 8–9 (pamphlet), War Savings Division Records.

16. Coercion files, Box 7, War Savings Division Records.

17. "Composite Questionnaire," August 17, 1918, 33, 140–142, 157, War Loan Organization Material, Box 1; Coercion files, Box 7; War Savings Division Records.

18. Vanderlip Speech to Magazine Publishers and Editors, July 17, 1918, Miscellaneous Letters A–3, Box 1; Conference of Members of Savings Division, April 19, 1919 (notes); Conference Material 1917–20,

Boxes 1 and 22, War Savings Division Records; House of Representatives, 65th Congress, 3rd session, House Document 1451, *Annual Report of the Secretary of The Treasury 1918*, 32–33; Vanderlip, *From Farm Boy to Financier*, 293. For war finance, see David M. Kennedy, *The First World War and American Society* (New York: Oxford University Press, 1980), 103–109.

19. "Conference with Federal Reserve Directors of Savings," December 30, 1918, 4–5 (bound volume); Carter Glass to Reverend Dear Sir, March 28, 1919; June 14, 1919; Glass to School Children, September 23, 1919; Miscellaneous Letters A–3, Box 1, Circular Letters Box 5, War Savings Division Records.

20. "Conference on War Savings with Savings Bank Society," May 19, 1919 (bound volume), Conference Materials, Box 1, War Savings Division Records.

21. "The Economic Program of the YMCA," "David G. Latshaw Suggested Sermon," "John Stapleton Suggested Sermon," "E. Hershey Sneath Suggested Sermon" (pamphlets), Box 1, War Savings Division Records.

22. Cardinal Gibbons to My Fellow Countrymen, February 12, 1919, Miscellaneous Letters A–3, War Savings Division Records.

23. "Conference of Federal Reserve Directors of Savings," December 30, 1918, 79–83; "School War Savings Plan for 1919" (leaflet); "Vacation Thrift Selling Contest" (leaflet); Box 24, War Savings Division Records.

24. Carter Glass to Ernest C. Hartwell, February 24, 1919; War Savings Bonds in Schools, file 47, Box 11; Orrin Lester to William M. Lewis, July 9, 1920, Conference file 77, Box 15, War Savings Division Records.

25. Orrin Lester to William M. Lewis, April 8, 1921, "History of School Thrift," Box 11; *Thrift in Schools: Outline of a Course of Study for Elementary Schools* (Washington, D. C., 1919); War Savings Division Records.

26. Conference of Members of Savings Division, April 10, 1919, 17–18, Conference Material, Box 1; Conference of Savings Division Officials, November 7–8, 1921, Box 15, War Savings Division Records.

27. Conference of Federal Reserve Directors of Savings, December 30, 1918, 228, 233; Conference on War Savings with Savings Banks Section, May 19, 1919, Conference Material, Box 1, War Savings Division Records.

28. William M. Lewis, "History of War Savings," March 26, 1921, War Loan Organization, Box 9, War Savings Division Records.

29. Warren G. Harding to John T. Wayland, January 12, 1921; Harding to Secretary Mellon, September 24, 1921; Mellon to Harding, September 29, 1921; Miscellaneous Letters A–3, Box 1 War Savings Division Records.

30. Andrew W. Mellon, "Thrift and Progress," *World's Work* 44 (May 1922), 36–39.

31. *New York Times*, January 23, 1921; Henry L. Doherty to D. F. Houston, January 24, 1921, Savings Campaign file 60, Box 13, War Savings Division Records; "The Menace of Thrift," *Nation* 112 (February 16, 1921), 256.

32. *New York Times*, January 18, 1921; *Literary Digest* 75 (December 9, 1922), 72; Henry Ford, *My Life and Work* (Garden City, NY: Doubleday, Page, 1922), 186–187.

33. Conference of Savings Division Officials, November 7–8, 1921; W. G. Brown to Lew Wallace, Jr., Protests from Bankers, file 123, Box 20, War Savings Division Records.

34. Complaints from Bankers, Senators, Congressmen, file 121, Box 19; Lew Wallace Jr. to Mrs. Ester Sandstrom, September 25, 1924; Suspension of Sales of Treasury Savings Certificates, file 146, Box 21, War Savings Division Records.

35. Conference of Directors, April 16, 1923, file 77, Box 15, War Savings Division Records.

CHAPTER 8

1. Ray Allen Billington, *The Protestant Crusade 1800–1860: A Study of the Origins of American Nativism* (New York: Macmillan, 1938), 132–135; Samuel C. Busey, *Immigration: Its Evils and Consequences* (New York: Dewitt & Davenport, 1856), 117–121.

2. 34th Congress, 1st session, House Report 359 (1856), 1, 118.

3. Reports of the Industrial Commission, *Immigration*, vol. 15 (Washington: Government Printing Office, 1902), 461–462. For a traditional view of German immigrants, see Benjamin Rush, *Essays* (Philadelphia: William Bradford, 1806), 225–248.

4. Scholarship begins with Mary Roberts Coolidge's sympathetic *Chinese Immigration* (New York: Henry Holt, 1909). Stuart Creghton Miller, in *The Unwelcome Immigrant: The American Image of the Chinese 1785–1882* (Berkeley: University of California Press, 1969), argues that Americans, not just Californians, were anti-Oriental. Gunther Barth, in *Bitter Strength: A History of the Chinese in the U.S. 1850–1870* (Cambridge: Harvard University Press, 1964), provides the best-written account but argues that the fact that Chinese were slave laborers explains their exclusion from the land of freedom. Alexander Saxton, in *The Indispensable Enemy: Labor and the Anti-Chinese Movement in California* (Berkeley: University of California Press, 1971), places blame squarely on trade unions.

5. Saxton, *The Indispensable Enemy*, 81.

6. California Senate Special Committee, *Chinese Immigration: Its Social, Moral and Political Effect* (Sacramento: State Printing Office, 1878), 47, 49, 260–262.

7. Ibid., 64.

8. 44th Congress, 2nd session, Senate Report 689, "Report of the Joint Special Committee to Investigate Chinese Immigration", 786, 778.

9. Ibid., 460, 450.

10. Ibid., 660–671, 723–728.

11. Ibid., 922, 952.

12. Ibid., 1138, 1067.

13. Ibid., iii–viii.

14. 45th Congress, 2nd session, *Senate Misc. Document 20*, "Views of the Late Oliver P. Morton on Chinese Immigration," 1–14.

15. *Congressional Record*, 47th Congress, 1st session, 1515–1523; Jack Chen, *The Chinese in America* (New York: Harper and Row, 1980), 151–168. American anti-Chinese riots were bloodier than those of Canada but never approached the 1911 Mexican massacre in Torreon, where more than 300 died. See Roger Daniel, ed., *Anti-Chinese Violence in North America* (New York, Arno, 1978), 239.

16. Thomas F. Turner, "Chinese and Japanese Labor in the Mountain and Pacific States," in *Immigration* Report of the United States Industrial Committee, vol. 15, 754; Roger Daniels, *The Politics of Prejudice: the Anti-Japanese Movement in California* (Berkeley: University of California Press, 1977), 19–21.

17. Saxton, *The Indispensable Enemy*, 248–249, 273.

18. John R. Commons, *Races and Immigrants in America* (New York: Macmillan, 1907), 78; John Higham, *Strangers in the Land: Patterns of American Nativism 1860–1925* (New York: Antheneum, 1965), 40–41, 101.

19. Henry Pratt Fairchild, *Immigration: A World Movement and its World Significance* (New York: Macmillan, 1913), 215–225.

20. Report of the U. S. Industrial Committee, *Immigration*, vol. 15, 53, 122; Robert Coit Chapin, *The Standard of Living Among Workingmen's Families in New York City* (New York: Charities Publication Committee, 1909), 235; Thomas Kessner, *The Golden Door: Italian and Jewish Immigrant Mobility in New York City 1880–1915* (New York: Oxford University Press, 1977), 151; Gary Ross Mormino, *Immigrants on the Hill: Italians in St. Louis 1882–1982* (Urbana: University of Illinois Press, 1986), 108–116.

21. Jacob A. Riis, *How the Other Half Lives: Studies among the Tenements of New York* ed. by Sam Bass Warner, Jr. (Cambridge: Harvard University Press, 1970), 70–71.

22. H. H. Ben-Sasson, *A History of the Jewish People* (Cambridge: Har-

vard University Press, 1976), 390–394; Higham, *Strangers in the Land*, 26–27, 160–161, 278.

23. 61st Congress 3rd session, *Senate Doc. 747*, "Reports of the Immigration Commission," (1911), 45–48; 67th Congress 1st session, *Senate Report 17*, "Emergency Immigration Legislation," (1921), 8–9; *Congressional Record*, 68th Congress 1st sess., vol 65, April 5–12, 1924, 5640–6263.

24. *Congressional Record*, April 8, 1924, 5888. For a biography of Fiorello La Guardia see Arthur Mann, *La Guardia: A Fighter Against His Times 1882–1933* (Philadelphia: J. B. Lippincott, 1959), or Thomas Kessner, *Fiorello H. La Guardia and the Making of Modern New York* (New York: McGraw-Hill, 1989).

25. Roy G. Blakey, "Foreword", *Annals of the American Academy of Political and Social Science* (January 1920) vol. 87, 2–3; T. N. Carver, "Thrift and the Standard of Living," *Journal of Political Economy* (November 1920), vol. 28, 284–286.

26. Edward A. Ross, *Standing Room Only* (New York: Century Company, 1927), 318–325.

27. "Differing Standards," *New York Times*, April 24, 1924, 18; Eliot Grinnell Mears, "California's Attitude Toward the Oriental," *Annals of the American Academy of Political and Social Science*, (November 1925), vol. 122, 202. For the Nordic theory and nativist racism, see Higham, *Strangers in the Land*.

CHAPTER 9

1. For the pre-war rebellion, see Henry May, *The End of Innocence* (New York: Alfred A. Knopf, 1959), 214–215; Frederick Lewis Allen, *Only Yesterday: An Informal History of the Nineteen-Twenties* (New York: Harper & Row, 1931), 188, 203; Warren I. Susman, *Culture as History: The Transformation of American History in the Twentieth Century* (New York: Pantheon Books, 1984), 111, 273–283; Richard W. Fox and T. J. Jackson Lears, *The Culture of Consumptionism: Critical Essays in American History 1880–1980* (New York: Pantheon Books, 1983), x–xiii.

2. Malcolm Cowley, *Exile's Return* (New York: Viking Press, 1961), 60–63.

3. Dane Yorke, "The Citadel of Thrift," *American Mercury* 11 (May 1927), 19–25; Chester T. Crowell, "Bank Day," *American Mercury* 20 (May 1930), 87–93; Charles L. Sanford, ed., *Benjamin Franklin and the American Character* (Boston: D. C. Heath, 1955), 60, 53.

4. Daniel Horowitz, *The Morality of Spending: Attitudes Toward the Consumer Society in America, 1875–1940* (Baltimore: Johns Hopkins Uni-

versity Press, 1985), 50–65, 97; "A Thriftless Generation," *Independent* 68 (June 2, 1910), 1254–1255; Frank Parker, "The Pay-as-you-use Idea," *Annals of American Academy of Political and Social Science* 196 (March 1938), 57–58; Robert S. and Helen Lynd, *Middletown: A Study in American Culture* (New York: Harcourt, Brace & Co., 1929), 46–47, 255.

5. Roland Marchand, *Advertising the American Dream: Making Way for Modernity, 1920–1940* (Berkeley: University of California Press, 1985), 6–24, 69, 158–160.

6. Thomas C. Cochran and William Miller, *The Age of Enterprise* (New York: Harper & Row, 1961), 311.

7. Daniel Horowitz, "Frugality or Comfort: Middle-Class Styles of Life in the Early Twentieth Century," *American Quarterly* 37 (Summer 1985), 239–259.

8. Mary Hinman Abel, *Successful Family Life on the Moderate Income* (Philadelphia: Lippincott, 1921), 175, 199–201, 205–208; "Editorial," *Journal of Home Economics* 17 (January 1925), 27–28.

9. C. W. Taber, *The Business of the Household* (Philadelphia: Lippincott, 1922), 6–7; Christine Frederick, *Efficient Housekeeping or Household Engineering* (Chicago: American School of Home Economics, 1925), 282.

10. Jane Addams, *Democracy and Social Ethics* (New York: Macmillan, 1902), 14, 31, 39–40, 149, 212–213; Allen F. Davis, *American Heroine: The Life and Legend of Jane Addams* (New York: Oxford University Press, 1973), 126–128. For the war against individualism, see Sidney Fine, *Laissez Faire and the General-Welfare State: A Study of Conflict in American Thought, 1865–1901* (Ann Arbor: University of Michigan, 1956). "Contempt" for Victorian thrift is expressed in the *Nation* 97 (July 10, 1913), 28–29.

11. Stow Persons, *American Minds: A History of Ideas* (New York: Henry Holt & Co., 1958), 252–264; John C. Burnham, "The New Psychology: From Narcissism to Social Control," in John Braeman et al., *Change and Continuity in Twentieth-Century America: The 1920s* (Columbus: Ohio State University Press, 1968), 351–398.

12. J. Laurence Laughlin, *The Elements of Political Economy* (New York: D. Appleton & Co., 1887), 348.

13. William Graham Sumner, *Folkways: A Study of the Sociological Importance of Usages, Manners, Customs, Mores, Morals* (Boston: Athenaeum Press, 1911), 33, 639, 652.

14. Lawrence A. Cremin, *The Transformation of the School* (New York: Alfred A. Knopf, 1964), 181–184; Harold Rugg, *The Teacher of Teachers* (New York: Harper & Brothers, 1952), 68–69, 70–74, 154–157, 224–225.

15. Robert Moats Miller, *Harry Emerson Fosdick: Preacher, Pastor, Prophet* (New York: Oxford University Press, 1985), 251, 275–280; Donald Meyer, *The Positive Thinkers* (Garden City: Doubleday & Company,

1965), 211–219; E. Brooks Holifield, *A History of Pastoral Care in America: From Salvation to Self-Realization* (Nashville: Abingdon Press, 1983), 219–221.

16. Edgar B. Wesley, *NEA: The First Hundred Years* (New York: Harper & Brothers, 1957), 240; Gary Scharnhorst, *Horatio Alger Jr.* (Boston: Twayne, 1980), 140–141.

17. Russell H. Conwell, *Acres of Diamonds* (New York: Harper & Brothers, 1915), 20, 58–59.

18. Paul A. Carter, *Another Part of the Twenties* (New York: Columbia University Press, 1977), 154; Meyer, *The Positive Thinkers*, 180–188; Richard M. Huber, *The American Idea of Success* (New York: McGraw-Hill, 1971).

CHAPTER 10

1. Edgar B. Wesley, *NEA: The First Hundred Years* (New York: Harper & Brothers, 1957), 243; *NEA Proceedings* (1933), 69; *New Republic* 72 (October 19, 1932), 245; Thurman Arnold, *The Folklore of Capitalism* (New Haven: Yale University Press, 1937), 124–125.

2. Arthur M. Schlesinger, Jr., *The Crisis of the Old Order* (Boston: Houghton Mifflin, 1957), 201–202; Richard H. Pells, *Radical Visions and American Dreams* (New York: Harper & Row, 1973), 71–75, 94–102; Robert B. Westbrook, "Tribune of the Technostructure: The Popular Economics of Stuart Chase," *American Quarterly* 32 (Fall 1980), 387–408; Stuart Chase, *The Economy of Abundance* (New York: Macmillan, 1934), 64–65, 275–279, 303; *NEA Proceedings* (1935), 526–534.

3. John Dewey, *Individualism Old and New* (New York: Minton, Balch & Co., 1930), 43–44, 109, 119; C. A. Bowers, *The Progressive Educator and the Depression: The Radical Years* (New York: Random House, 1969), 1–33, 44–49; *The Social Frontier* (October 1934), 1.

4. T. Swann Harding, "What This Country Needs," *The Social Frontier* 5 (June 1939), 268–271.

5. William T. Foster & Waddill Catchings, "Riotous Savings," *Atlantic Monthly* (November 1930), 667–670; Arthur M. Schlesinger, Jr., *The Politics of Upheaval* (Boston: Houghton Mifflin, 1960), 237–241.

6. For the public Keynes, see R. F. Harrod, *The Life of John Maynard Keynes* (New York: Harcourt Brace, 1952), 172–194, 405–407. For an amoral view, see Charles H. Hession, *John Maynard Keynes* (New York: Macmillan, 1984), or Robert Skidelsky, *John Maynard Keynes: Hopes Betrayed, 1883–1920*, vol. 1 (New York: Viking, 1986); Robert Lekachman, *The Age of Keynes* (New York: Random House, 1966), 78–111.

7. William L. Nunn, "Revolution in the Idea of Thrift," *Annals of American Academy of Political and Social Science* 196 (March 1938), 54.

8. Robert S. and Helen Lynd, *Middletown in Transition* (New York: Harcourt, Brace & Co., 1937), 476–481.

9. Ibid., 479.

10. "Thrift and Money Management," *Journal of Home Economics* 27 (January 1935), 36–37.

11. James MacGregor Burns, *Roosevelt: The Lion and the Fox* (New York: Harcourt, Brace & World, 1956), 329–336; Lekachman, *The Age of Keynes*, 112–114; Marriner S. Eccles, *Beckoning Frontiers* (New York: Alfred A. Knopf, 1951), 96–99; Hadley Cantril & Mildred Strunk, *Public Opinion 1935–1946* (Princeton: Princeton University Press, 1951), 58.

12. John Kenneth Galbraith, *A Life in Our Times* (Boston: Houghton Mifflin, 1981), 67–69, 124–173; Herbert Stein, *The Fiscal Revolution in America* (Chicago: University of Chicago Press, 1969), 162–163.

13. Stein, *Fiscal Revolution in America*, 91–130, 167–168; Robert M. Collins, *The Business Response to Keynes, 1929–1964* (New York: Columbia University Press, 1981), 12–13, 44.

14. Harold F. Clark, "Thrift and National Welfare," *School and Society* 52 (November 2, 1940), 414–417.

15. Thomas C. Cochran and William Miller, *The Age of Enterprise: A Social History of Industrial America* (New York: Harper & Row, 1942, 1961), 354–358.

CHAPTER 11

1. Robert Lekachman, *The Age of Keynes* (New York: Random House, 1966), 144–153; John Maynard Keynes, *How To Pay for the War* (London: Macmillan, 1940), 9, 10, 17, 42.

2. John Kenneth Galbraith, *A Life in Our Times: Memoirs* (Boston: Houghton Mifflin, 1981), 172–173.

3. John M. Blum, *From the Morgenthau Diaries* (Boston: Houghton Mifflin, 1967), 17–18.

4. *Press Conferences of F.D.R.* (New York: Da Capo Press, 1972), 50–51; Samuel I. Rosenman, *The Public Papers and Addresses of Franklin D. Roosevelt* (New York: Harper & Brothers, 1950), vol. X, 139–140; vol. XI, 216–224; vol. XII, 380.

5. Savings Bond Promotions, Boxes 2, 5, Treasury Department, Record Group 56, National Archives; *NEA Proceedings* 79 (1941), 67–68; Homer W. Anderson, "The Significance of the Home Front in the War Savings Program," *Journal of Educational Sociology* 16 (January 1943), 273–278.

6. Robert M. Collins, *The Business Response to Keynes, 1929–1964* (New York: Columbia University Press, 1981), 99; Robert R. Nathan, *Mobilizing for Abundance* (New York: McGraw-Hill, 1944), 66, 95–98, 199, 204–205.

7. Lester V. Chandler, *Inflation in the United States 1940–1948* (New York: Harper & Brothers, 1951), 2–9, 216–217; William E. Leuchtenburg, *A Troubled Feast: American Society Since 1945* (Boston: Little, Brown and Company, 1973), 61–79; Frances Lomas Feldman, "A New Look at the Family and Its Money," *Journal of Home Economics* 45 (December 1957), 769, 772.

8. *New York Times Magazine*, January 17, 1954, 60; October 19, 1958.

9. J. K. Lasser & Sylvia F. Porter, *Managing Your Money* (New York: Henry Holt & Co., 1953), 12; Augustus H. Smith, Gladys Bahr, Fred T. Wilhelms, *Your Personal Economics: An Introduction to Consumer Education* (New York: McGraw-Hill, 1953), 81–82.

10. Savings Bond Promotions, Boxes 4, 5, Treasury Department, Record Group 56, National Archives.

11. *New York Times Magazine*, December 1, 1957, 108; *New York Times*, May 3, 1987, sect. 4, letters.

12. David Riesman, Nathan Glazer, and Reuel Denney, *The Lonely Crowd: A Study of the Changing American Character* (New Haven: Yale University Press, 1950), 30, 34.

13. C. Wright Mills, *White Collar* (New York: Oxford University Press, 1951), 235–238.

14. Richard Hofstadter, William Miller, and Daniel Aaron, *The American Republic*, vol. II (Englewood Cliffs: Prentice-Hall, 1959), 586–588.

15. Paul A. Samuelson, *Economics: An Introductory Analysis* (New York: McGraw-Hill, 1948), 270–272.

16. Stephen E. Ambrose, *Eisenhower: The President* (New York: Simon & Schuster, 1984), 460, 158–159; Herbert Stein, *The Fiscal Revolution in America* (Chicago: University of Chicago Press, 1969), 281–308.

17. John Kenneth Galbraith, *The Affluent Society* (Cambridge: Riverside Press, 1958), 308–311.

18. Irene Oppenheim, *Management of the Modern Home* (New York: Macmillan, 1972), 149, 37–49; William J. Bennett & Edwin J. Delattre, "Moral Education in the School," *Public Interest* (Winter 1978), 81–98; Dwight Boyd & Deanne Bogden, "Something Clarified, Nothing of Value: A Rhetorical Critique of Values Clarification," *Educational Theory* 34 (Summer 1984), 287–300; Irene S. Pyszkowski, "Moral Values and the Schools—Is There a Way Out of the Maze?" *Education* 107 (Fall 1986), 41–48.

19. See the Lester Rand Youth Polls, *Wall Street Journal*, October 17,

1974, 1; and *U. S. News and World Report* 77 (November 18, 1974), 124; *New York Times*, May 3, 1987, sect. 4, letters.

20. James U. McNeal, *Children as Consumers* (Lexington, MA:D. C. Heath, 1987), 4, 12, 32–34, 62.

21. Robert B. Avery, et al., "Survey of Consumer Finances, 1983: A Second Look," *Federal Reserve Bulletin* (December 1984), 858, 862–864; "Changes in Consumer Installment Debt: Evidence from 1983 and 1986," *Federal Reserve Bulletin* (October 1987), 763.

22. Quoted by Howard Flieger, "Paying the Piper," *U. S. News and World Report* 77 (November 18, 1974), 124. From *Collected Poems*, Second Edition by Conrad Aiken. Copyright © 1953, 1970 by Conrad Aiken. Reprinted by permission of Oxford University Press, Inc.

CHAPTER 12

1. For an insider's view of Reagan as a reluctant budget balancer, see David A. Stockman, *The Triumph of Politics: How the Reagan Revolution Failed* (New York: Harper & Row, 1986), 11, 349; Phillip Longman, "The Fall of the Idea of Thrift," *Washington Monthly* 16 (January 1985), 13.

2. Robert Lekachman, *The Age of Keynes* (New York: Random House, 1966), 270–284.

3. Herbert Stein, *The Fiscal Revolution in America* (Chicago: University of Chicago Press, 1969), 374–382, 412–417; Robert M. Collins, *The Business Response to Keynes, 1929–1964* (New York: Columbia University Press, 1981), 173–194.

4. Paul Samuelson, *Economics*, 7th ed. (New York: McGraw-Hill, 1967), 342–343; Lester Thurow, *The Zero Sum Society* (New York: Basic Books, 1980), 42–47.

5. School Savings Program, Box 4, Savings Bond Promotions, Treasury Department, Record Group 56, National Archives.

6. School banks faded away without public discussion.

7. Thurow, *The Zero Sum Solution: Building a World-Class American Economy* (New York: Simon & Schuster, 1985), 208–214.

8. David E. Shi, *The Simple Life: Plain Living and High Thinking in American Culture* (New York: Oxford University Press, 1985), 264–272.

9. Ronald Reagan, *A Time for Choosing: The Speeches of Ronald Reagan 1961–1982* (Chicago: Regnery Gateway, 1983), 233.

10. Milton and Rose Friedman, *Free to Choose: A Personal Statement* (New York: Harcourt Brace, 1980); Rich Thomas, "The Magic of Reaganomics," *Newsweek* (December 26, 1988), 40–44; William Greider, *Secrets of the Temple: How the Federal Reserve Runs the Country* (New York: Simon & Schuster, 1987), 379, 418.

11. George Gilder, *Wealth and Poverty* (New York: Basic Books Inc., 1981), 51, 68, 73, 83.

12. Stockman, *The Triumph of Politics*, 321–322, 396; Alfred L. Malabre, Jr., *Beyond Our Means: How America's Long Years of Debt, Deficits and Reckless Borrowing Now Threaten to Overwhelm Us* (New York: Random House, 1987), 7, 77–78, 80.

13. Peter G. Peterson, "The Morning After," *Atlantic* 260 (October 1987), 50.

14. John Kenneth Galbraith, *Economics in Perspective* (Boston: Houghton Mifflin, 1987), 271–276, 298; Paul E. Peterson, "The New Politics of Deficits," *Political Science Quarterly* 100 (Winter 1985–86), 574–601.

15. Felix Rohatyn, "On the Brink," *New York Review of Books* 34 (June 11, 1987), 3.

16. Susan Lee and Tatiana Pouschini, "Are We a Nation of Spendthrifts?" *Forbes* 136 (December 16, 1985), 128–134.

17. Thurow, *Zero Sum Solution*, 29–30, 208–214.

18. Robert N. Bellah, *Tokugawa Religion: The Values of Pre-industrial Japan* (Glencoe, IL: The Free Press, 1957), 112–113, 126–130, 195–196.

19. Toshiyuki Mizoguchi, *Personal Savings and Consumption in Postwar Japan* (Tokyo: Kinokuniya Bookstore Co., 1970), 256. However, economists and sociologists certainly question any direct relationship between Japanese values and their savings rate. See Kazuo Sato, "Savings and Investment" in Kozo Yamamura & Yasukichi Yasuba, *The Political Economy of Japan*, vol. I (Stanford: Stanford University Press, 1987), 140; and Nathan Glazer, "Social and Cultural Factors in Japanese Economic Growth," in Hugh Patrick & Henry Rosovsky, *Asia's New Giant: How the Japanese Economy Works* (Washington: Brookings Institution, 1976), 856–859.

20. Harold L. Dayton, Jr., *Your Money: The Biblical Guide to Earning, Saving, Spending, Investing, Giving* (Wheaton: Tyndale House, 1979); Ron Blue, *Master Your Money* (Nashville: Thomas Nelson, 1986); Larry Burkett, *Your Finances in Changing Times* (Chicago: Moody Press, 1982); Irving Kristol, "Skepticism, Meliorism, and the Public Interest," *The Public Interest* (Fall 1985), 39.

21. Peter T. Blanchard, Massachusetts Bankers Association, to author, July 16, 1987; Lee Bryan Mulder, PEP, to author, July 16, 1987; Sue L. Hickey, Massachusetts Office of the Commissioner of Banks, to author, August 3, 1987.

22. David M. Reimers, *Still the Golden Door* (New York: Columbia University Press, 1985), 109–113.

23. Ibid., 164–169; Bureau of the Census, *Household Wealth and Asset Ownership: 1984* (Washington, D. C.: Government Printing Office,

1986), 1, 5. Comparative rates of national saving and investing are charted by Lawrence Summers and Chris Carroll in "Why is U. S. National Saving So Low?" *Brookings Papers on Economic Activity* 2 (1987), 634.

24. Savings rates may be found in government periodicals, U. S. Department of Commerce *Survey of Current Business*, or in the *Economic Report of the President, February, 1988*, 278. The 15 percent rate is taken from Raymond W. Goldsmith, *A Study of Savings in the United States* vol. I (Princeton: Princeton University Press, 1955), 241.

25. Steven V. Roberts, "Phil Gramm's Crusade Against the Deficit," *New York Times Magazine*, March 30, 1986, 20, 40.

26. Peterson, "The Morning After," *Atlantic* October 1987, 60–66; *Wall Street Journal*, November 19, 1987, 58.

27. *Budget of the United States Government 1989* (Washington, D. C.: Government Printing Office, 1988), 5–157; *Economic Report of the President, February 1988*, 3–10, 100–101.

28. *Newsweek*, December 26, 1988, 41–44; *Wall Street Journal*, December 14, 1988, A16.

29. *New York Times*, July 30, 1989, E4; December 17, 1989, F1; The lively debate among economists—Franco Modigliani and Robert Solow versus Robert Eisner—may be followed in the *New York Times* letters, February 19 and March 12, 1989; and in the *New York Review of Books*, September 28, 1989, 73–74.

Selected Bibliography

MANUSCRIPTS

Savings Bond Promotions, Treasury Department. Record Group 56. National Archives.

War Savings Division Records. Bureau of Public Debt. Record Group 53. National Archives.

PUBLIC DOCUMENTS

California Senate Special Committee. *Chinese Immigration: Its Social, Moral and Political Effect*. Sacramento: State Printing Office, 1878.

U.S. Bureau of the Census. *Household Wealth and Asset Ownership: 1984*. Washington, D. C.: Government Printing Office, 1986.

U.S. House of Representatives. 51st Congress, 1st session. *House Executive Document 2729*. "Report of U.S. Bureau of Education."

U.S. Industrial Committee. *Immigration*, vol. 15. Washington, D. C.: Government Printing Office, 1902.

U.S. Senate. 44th Congress, 2nd session. *Senate Report 689*. "Report of the Joint Special Committee to Investigate Chinese Immigration."

————. 45th Congress, 2nd session. *Senate Misc. Document 20*. "Views of the Late Oliver P. Morton on Chinese Immigration."

ARTICLES

Anderson, Homer W. "The Significance of the Home Front in the War Savings Program." *Journal of Educational Sociology* 16 (January 1943), 273–278.

Avery, Robert B., et al. "Survey of Consumer Finances, 1983: A Second Look." *Federal Reserve Bulletin* (December 1984), 858–864.

Blakey, Roy G. "The New American Thrift." *Annals of the American Academy of Social and Political Science* 87 (January 1920), 1–3.

Carver, T. N. "Thrift and the Standard of Living." *Journal of Political Economy* 28 (November 1920), 784–786.

Faler, Paul. "Cultural Aspects of the Industrial Revolution: Lynn, Massachusetts, Shoemakers and Industrial Morality, 1826–1860." *Labor History* 15 (Summer 1974), 367–394.

Foster, George M. "Peasant Society and the Image of Limited Good." *American Anthropologist* 67 (April 1965), 293–315.

Foster, William T. and Waddill Catchings. "Riotous Savings." *Atlantic Monthly* 146 (November 1930), 667–672.

Higgs, Robert. "Accumulation of Property by Southern Blacks Before World War I." *American Economic Review* 72 (September 1982), 725–737.

Horowitz, Daniel. "Frugality or Comfort: Middle-Class Styles of Life in the Early Twentieth Century." *American Quarterly* 73 (Summer 1985), 239–259.

Litto, Frederic M. "Addison's *Cato* in the Colonies." *William and Mary Quarterly* 23 (July 1966), 430–449.

Longman, Phillip. "The Fall of the Idea of Thrift." *Washington Monthly* 16 (January 1985), 12–22.

Mears, Eliot Grinnell. "California's Attitude Toward the Oriental." *Annals of the American Academy of Political and Social Science* 122 (November 1925), 199–213.

Morgan, Edmund S. "The Puritan Ethic and the American Revolution." *William and Mary Quarterly* 24 (January 1967), 3–15.

Nunn, William L. "Revolution in the Idea of Thrift." *Annals of the American Academy of Political and Social Science* 196 (March 1938), 52–56.

Peterson, Peter G. "The Morning After." *Atlantic* 260 (October 1987), 43–50.

Roberts, Steven V. "Phil Gramm's Crusade Against the Deficit." *New York Times Magazine* (March 30, 1986), 20–23.

Rohatyn, Felix. "On the Brink." *New York Review of Books* 34 (June 11, 1987), 3–4.

Smith, Timothy L. "Protestant Schooling and American Nationality, 1800–1850." *Journal of American History* 53 (March 1967), 679–695.

Summers, Lawrence and Chris Carroll. "Why is U.S. National Saving So Low?" *Brookings Papers on Economic Activity*, no. 2 (1987), 607–635.

Thomas, Rich. "Saving: Not the American Way." *Newsweek* 115 (January 9, 1990), 44–45.
Westbrook, Robert B. "Tribune of the Technostructure: The Popular Economics of Stuart Chase." *American Quarterly* 32 (Fall 1980), 387–408.
Woodward, C. Vann. "The Southern Ethic in a Puritan World." *William and Mary Quarterly* 25 (July 1968), 343–370.

BOOKS

Abel, Mary Hinman. *Successful Family Life on the Moderate Income.* Philadelphia: Lippincott, 1921.
Alger, Horatio, Jr. *Ragged Dick.* Edited by Carl Bode. New York: Penguin Books, 1985.
Barth, Gunther. *Bitter Strength: A History of the Chinese in the U.S. 1850–1870.* Cambridge: Harvard University Press, 1964.
Bellah, Robert N. *Tokugawa Religion: The Values of Pre-industrial Japan.* Glencoe, IL: Free Press, 1957.
Ben-Sasson, H. H. *A History of the Jewish People.* Cambridge: Harvard University Press, 1976.
Bowers, C. A. *The Progressive Educator and the Depression: The Radical Years.* New York: Random House, 1969.
Braudel, Fernand. *Civilization and Capitalism.* New York: Harper & Row, 1982.
Breen, T. H. *Tobacco Culture: The Mentality of the Great Tidewater Planters on the Eve of the Revolution.* Princeton: Princeton University Press, 1985.
Carver, Thomas Nixon. *War Thrift.* New York: Oxford University Press, 1919.
Collins, Robert M. *The Business Response to Keynes, 1929–1964.* New York: Columbia University Press, 1981.
Cooper, Thomas. *Lectures on the Elements of Political Economy.* Columbia: McMorris & Wilson, 1828.
Cowley, Malcolm. *Exile's Return.* New York: Viking Press 1961.
Cremin, Lawrence A. *The Transformation of the School.* New York: Alfred A. Knopf, 1964.
Crowley, J. E. *This Sheba, Self: The Conceptualization of Economic Life in Eighteenth Century America.* Baltimore: Johns Hopkins University Press, 1979.
Doerflinger, Thomas M. *A Vigorous Spirit of Enterprise: Merchants & Economic Development in Revolutionary Philadelphia.* Chapel Hill: University of North Carolina Press, 1986.

Faler, Paul. *Mechanics and Manufacturers in the Early Industrial Revolution: Lynn, Massachusetts 1780–1860*. Albany: State University of New York Press, 1981.

Fei, Hsiao-Tung and Chih-I Chang. *Earthbound in China: A Study of Rural Economy in Yunnan*. Chicago: University of Chicago Press, 1945.

Fleming, Walter L. *The Freedmen's Savings Bank*. Chapel Hill: University of North Carolina Press, 1927.

Foster, Stephen. *Their Solitary Way: The Puritan Social Ethic in the First Century of Settlement in New England*. New Haven: Yale University Press, 1971.

Fox, Richard W. and T. J. Jackson Lears. *The Culture of Consumptionism: Critical Essays in American History*. New York: Pantheon Books, 1983.

Franklin, Benjamin. *The Papers of Benjamin Franklin*. Edited by Leonard W. Labaree. New Haven: Yale University Press, 1963.

Frazier, E. Franklin. *Black Bourgeoisie: The Rise of a New Middle Class*. New York: Free Press, 1957.

Frederick, Christine. *Efficient Housekeeping or Household Engineering*. Chicago: American School of Home Economics, 1925.

Friedman, Benjamin. *Day of Reckoning: The Consequences of American Economic Policy under Reagan and After*. New York: Random House, 1988.

Galbraith, John Kenneth. *The Affluent Society*. Cambridge: Riverside Press, 1958.

———. *A Life in Our Times*. Boston: Houghton Mifflin, 1981.

Genovese, Eugene D. *Roll, Jordan Roll: The World the Slaves Made*. New York: Random House, 1974.

Gilder, George. *Wealth and Poverty*. New York: Basic Books, 1981.

Goldsmith, Raymond W. *A Study of Savings in the United States*. Princeton: Princeton University Press, 1955.

Greider, William. *Secrets of the Temple: How the Federal Reserve Runs the Country*. New York: Simon & Schuster, 1987.

Greven, Philip. *The Protestant Temperament: Patterns of Child-Rearing, Religious Experience, and Self in Early America*. New York: Alfred A. Knopf, 1977.

Hale, Sarah J. *Keeping House and House Keeping: A Story of Domestic Life*. New York: Harper & Brothers, 1845.

Harrod, R. F. *The Life of John Maynard Keynes*. New York: Harcourt Brace, 1952.

Hession, Charles H. *John Maynard Keynes*. New York: Macmillan, 1984.

Higham, John. *Strangers in the Land: Patterns of American Nativism 1860–1925*. New York: Atheneum, 1965.

Himmelfarb, Gertrude. *The Idea of Poverty: England in the Early Industrial Age*. New York: Alfred A. Knopf, 1984.

Holifield, E. Brooks. *A History of Pastoral Care in America: From Salvation to Self-Realization*. Nashville: Abingdon Press, 1983.

Horowitz, Daniel. *The Morality of Spending: Attitudes toward the Consumer Society in America, 1875–1940*. Baltimore: Johns Hopkins University Press, 1985.

Keyes, Emerson. *A History of Savings Banks in the United States 1816–1874*. New York: Bradford Rhodes, 1876.

Keynes, John Maynard. *How to Pay for the War*. London: Macmillan, 1940.

Laughlin, J. Laurence. *The Elements of Political Economy*. New York: D. Appleton, 1887.

Laurie, Bruce. *Working People of Philadelphia 1800–1850*. Philadelphia: Temple University Press, 1980.

Leidecker, Kurt F. *Yankee Teacher: The Life of William Torrey Harris*. New York: Philosophical Library, 1946.

Lekachman, Robert. *The Age of Keynes*. New York: Random House, 1966.

Lintner, John. *Mutual Savings Banks in the Savings and Mortgage Markets*. Boston: Harvard Graduate School of Business Administration, 1948.

Lynd, Robert S. and Helen Lynd. *Middletown: A Study in American Culture*. New York: Harcourt Brace, 1929.

McNeal, James U. *Children as Consumers*. Lexington, MA: D. C. Heath, 1987.

McWhiney, Grady. *Cracker Culture: Celtic Ways in the Old South*. Tuscaloosa: University of Alabama Press, 1988.

Malabre, Alfred L. Jr. *Beyond Our Means: How America's Long Years of Debt, Deficits and Reckless Borrowing Now Threaten to Overwhelm Us*. New York: Random House, 1987.

Mann, Arthur. *La Guardia: A Fighter Against His Times 1882–1933*. Philadelphia: J. B. Lippincott, 1959.

Marchand, Roland. *Advertising the American Dream: Making Way for Modernity, 1920–1940*. Berkeley: University of California Press, 1985.

Miller, Robert Moats. *Harry Emerson Fosdick: Preacher, Pastor, Prophet*. New York: Oxford University Press, 1985.

Oppenheim, Irene. *Management of the Modern Home*. New York: Macmillan, 1972.

Osthaus, Carl R. *Freedman, Philanthropy and Fraud: A History of the Freedman's Saving Bank*. Urbana: University of Illinois Press, 1976.

Peacham, Henry. *The Worth of a Peny or a Caution to Keep Money*. London: S. Griffen, 1664.

Pells, Richard H. *Radical Visions and American Dreams*. New York: Harper & Row, 1973.

Pessen, Edward. *Riches, Class and Power Before the Civil War*. Lexington, MA: D. C. Heath, 1973.

Phillips, Willard. *A Manual of Political Economy*. Boston: Hilliard, Gray, 1828.

Ravitch, Diane. *The Great School Wars: New York City, 1805–1973*. New York: Basic Books, 1974.

Raymond, Daniel. *The Elements of Political Economy*. Baltimore: F. Lucas Jr., 1823.

Redlich, Fritz. *The Molding of American Banking*. New York: Hafner Publishing, 1951.

Riesman, David, Nathan Glazer, and Revel Denny. *The Lonely Crowd: A Study of the Changing American Character*. New Haven: Yale University Press, 1950.

Riis, Jacob A. *How the Other Half Lives: Studies Among the Tenements of New York*. Edited by Sam Bass Warner, Jr. Cambridge: Harvard University Press, 1976.

Robinson, Edward L. *One Hundred Years of Savings Banking*. American Banking Association, 1917.

Rogers, Sherbrooke. *Sarah Josepha Hale: A New England Pioneer*. Grantham, N. H.: Thompson and Ruther, 1985.

Ross, Edward A. *Standing Room Only*. New York: Century Company, 1927.

Samuelson, Paul A. *Economics: An Introductory Analysis*. New York: McGraw-Hill, 1948.

Saxton, Alexander. *The Indispensable Enemy: Labor and the Anti-Chinese Movement in California*. Berkeley: University of California Press, 1971.

Schlesinger, Arthur M. Jr. *The Crisis of the Old Order*. Boston: Houghton Mifflin, 1957.

Semmel, Bernard. *The Methodist Revolution*. New York: Basic Books, 1973.

Shi, David E. *The Simple Life: Plain Living and High Thinking in American Culture*. New York: Oxford University Press, 1985.

Skidelsky, Robert. *John Maynard Keynes: Hopes Betrayed, 1883–1920*. New York: Viking, 1986.

Smith, Adam. *An Inquiry into the Nature and Causes of the Wealth of Nations*. Edited by Edwin Cannan. Chicago: University of Chicago Press, 1976.

Steffen, Charles G. *The Merchants of Baltimore: Workers and Politics in the Age of Revolution 1763–1812*. Urbana: University of Illinois Press, 1984.

Stein, Herbert. *The Fiscal Revolution in America*. Chicago: University of Chicago Press, 1969.

Stockman, David A. *The Triumph of Politics: How the Reagan Revolution Failed*. New York: Harper & Row, 1986.

Straus, Simon W. *History of the Thrift Movement in America*. Philadelphia: J. B. Lippincott, 1920.

Susman, Warren I. *Culture as History: The Transformation of American History in the Twentieth Century*. New York: Pantheon Books, 1984.

Taber, C. W. *The Business of the Household*. Philadelphia: J. B. Lippincott, 1922.

Thernstrom, Stephan. *Poverty and Progress: Social Mobility in a Nineteenth Century City*. Cambridge: Harvard University Press, 1964.

Thompson, E. P. *The Making of the English Working Class*. New York: Pantheon Books, 1964.

Thurow, Lester. *The Zero Sum Society*. New York: Basic Books, 1980.

———. *The Zero Sum Solution: Building a World-Class American Economy*. New York: Simon & Schuster, 1985.

Tocqueville, Alexis de. *Democracy in America*. Edited by J. P. Mayer. New York: Harper & Row, 1966.

Washington, Booker T. *Character Building*. New York: Doubleday, 1902.

Wayland, Francis. *The Elements of Moral Science*. Edited by Joseph L. Blau. Cambridge: Harvard University Press, 1963.

Weber, Max. *The Protestant Ethic and the Spirit of Capitalism*. translated by Talcott Parsons. New York: Scribner's, 1958.

Westerhoff, John A. *McGuffey and his Readers: Piety, Morality, and Education in Nineteenth-Century America*. Nashville: Abingdon, 1978.

Index

ABOUT THE AUTHOR

DAVID M. TUCKER was born in rural Arkansas in 1937 and learned thrift in small towns not unlike those of nineteenth-century America. He earned history degrees from the College of the Ozarks, Oklahoma State, and the University of Iowa.

Since 1965 Professor Tucker has taught American history at Memphis State University and has written six books. His subjects have ranged from African-American business and religion, to urban reform politics, the reputation of Arkansas, and a history of vegetable gardening.